Nightmare

A Suspense Play

Norman Robbins

Samuel French – London
New York – Sydney – Toronto – Hollywood

For my wife, Ailsa

nightmare (nīt mār), n A terrifying dream, impression or experience accompanied with a feeling of suffocation and inability to move or speak.

NIGHTMARE

First performed at the Oast Theatre, Tonbridge, on October 24th, 1987 with the following cast of characters:

Doris Meacham	Rita Carpenter
Katherine Willis	Karen Elves
Dr Andrew Thorne	John Taylor
Michael Willis	Andrew Rayfield
Raymond Shapley	John Rutherford
Marion Bishop	Joan Lloyd
Laura Vinnecombe	Valerie Armstrong

The play directed by Ken Banister

The action of the play takes place in the living-room of Marion Bishop's home, Moor View, an isolated house on the edge of Barrowdale Moor, two miles from the village of Hanbury.

ACT I

SCENE 1   A Saturday morning in mid-September
SCENE 2   Two weeks later
SCENE 3   Ten days later, evening

ACT II

SCENE 1   Later that evening
SCENE 2   Four days later, morning
SCENE 3   The following day, evening

Time—the present

**Other plays and pantomimes by
Norman Robbins
published by Samuel French Ltd**

Aladdin
Ali Baba and the Forty Thieves
Babes in the Wood
Cinderella
Dick Whittington
The Grand Old Duke of York
Hickory Dickory Dock
Humpty Dumpty
Jack and the Beanstalk
The Late Mrs Early
Pull The Other One
Puss in Boots
Rumpelstiltzkin
Sing a Song of Sixpence
Slaughterhouse
Sleeping Beauty
Snow White
Tiptoe Through the Tombstones
(*the sequel to* A Tomb With a View)
Tom, the Piper's Son
A Tomb With a View
Wedding of the Year
The Wonderful Story of Mother Goose

ACT I

The living-room of Marion Bishop's home. A hot Saturday morning in mid-September

The room is bright and cheerful, reflecting the romantic writings of its owner. In the back wall, there are two large windows, one L, the other R. Both look out on to a breathtaking view of the moor. Between the two windows is the front door, solid and heavy. When the door is open, one can see into a large porch constructed of stone and glassed wooden frames. This is open to the L. Inside the porch are coat hooks, a small table with a ceramic vase filled with an arrangement of twigs and dried flowers. There are a pair of galoshes or Wellington boots, a trowel and plant pots, an apple box and an umbrella stand. Tendrils of creeper can be seen hanging outside the glassed upper portion of the porch, and of course, the view of the moor. Beneath the window L is a polished drop-leaf table, partially covered by a crocheted cloth in the centre of it; a bowl of fresh roses stands on it. Two chairs are also present, one at each side of the table. Attractive brocade curtains hang at the windows. Beneath the window R, is a chest of drawers, obviously valuable. A telephone stands on top of this, plus a notepad, pen, address book and telephone directory. There is also a small lamp and a statuette. UR, is a second door which leads to the rest of the house. Below the door is a large Welsh dresser, its shelves laden with stoneware crockery. Its working surface holds a silver tray with several decanters and a selection of glasses, a copper bowl containing twigs and cut flowers, and a glass bowl of fresh fruit. Below the dresser is a dining-chair. Opposite this, on the wall L, is a built-in unit. The lower half is filled with books, and a small television set, facing US and flanked by ornaments, stands on top. On the wall behind this, hangs a painting of the moor. US of the unit is the fireplace, possibly a reproduction Adam, its mantle holding a collection of small objects d'art. In front of the hearth is a small rug. On the hearth, polished-brass fire-irons and a china cat. Over the fireplace is another painting of the moor. US of the fireplace is another built-in unit. The lower half is filled with books, plus a stack of long-playing records. A modern record-player stands on top of the unit. The wall above holds a small collection of framed pictures. Angled towards the fireplace is a large, comfortable settee with bright cushions. A low coffee table is set in front of this. By the US arm of the settee is a small wine table. On this stands a reading lamp and a book. The floor is thickly carpeted

When the CURTAIN *rises, the room is empty and the front door is open. Bright sunlight fills the room. After a moment, the sound of a woman's voice is heard, off*

Doris (*off; cheerily*) Morning, Michael.

A moment later, Doris Meacham passes the window L and enters the front door. She is a chubby little woman of fifty or so. She wears a floral-print dress and sensible flat shoes. She carries a large box of groceries

(*Calling towards the door R*) Oo-oo. Groceries. (*She deposits the box on the table L, and gives a sigh of relief. Taking an order book from the box she quickly checks off the list against the goods, then noticing no-one has arrived in answer to her call, calls again*) Katherine? Are you there, love?

The door R opens, and Katherine Willis enters looking slightly flushed. She is a plain-looking woman of twenty-four, wearing a skirt and blouse with a white apron tied about her waist

Katherine (*apologetically*) Sorry to have kept you, Mrs Meacham. I was taking some tea upstairs.

Doris (*easily*) Oh, that's all right, love. I'm not in any hurry. How is she today? Feeling any better?

Katherine Oh, yes. I think so. She seems bright enough. Dr Thorne's with her now.

Doris (*nodding*) Noticed his car when I drove up. (*She chuckles*) If I'd known he was on his way here, I'd have asked him to drop the groceries in for you. (*Quickly*) Not that I mind though. Don't get me wrong. (*She smiles*) Gives me a chance to get out of the shop. Let his lordship do a bit of work for a change, eh?

Katherine (*smiling*) It is good of you to bring everything, Mrs Meacham. I must admit I wasn't looking forward to carrying it all from the village. Not in this weather. (*She sighs deeply*) Isn't it hot?

Doris (*nodding*) Some sort of freak heatwave, according to the forecast. Hottest day of the year, yesterday was, he said, but if you want my opinion, today's going to be hotter. (*Nodding to the window R*) Still, there's some people finding pleasure in it.

Katherine (*following her glance*) Michael, you mean? (*She smiles*) Yes. He's in his element out there. If things had been different . . .

Doris (*firmly*) Well, they weren't, dear, and there's nothing anyone can do about it. (*Reassuringly*) But he's a good boy. Everyone thinks the world of him and don't you forget it. He's doing a wonderful job with that bottom end. Cleared right round that old summer-house.

Katherine (*smiling*) Yes. It is coming on, I must admit.

Doris Used to be a lovely garden, that did. Croquet lawn, fruit trees, vegetable patches, herb garden. Oh, everything. Even had its own well. Mind you, that was boarded over when they had the mains put in, but if ever there's a water shortage, you can bet they'll still find a drop or two there. Oh, and the parties they used to have. I had my very first strawberries out here, you know. Strawberries, sugar and cream—and scented tea in a bone china cup. (*She smiles at the memory*)

Katherine (*realizing*) Oh. Would you care for a cup now? I've only just made it.

Doris (*shaking her head*) Oh, no. No, thanks. I'd better be going. I told him I wouldn't be long.

Katherine It won't take a minute. I've only to pour it.

Doris (*giving in*) Well, all right then. You've twisted my arm. Milk and two sugars.

Katherine smiles and exits R

Doris moves to the settee and sits down

After a few moments, Katherine enters with a tray. On it are two cups and saucers and a plate of biscuits. She crosses to the coffee table and deposits the tray

Katherine Here we are. I've brought a few biscuits too. (*She sits beside Doris*)

Doris (*helping herself to a cup and sipping*) Lovely. It was old Mr Harrison laid it all out, you know.

Katherine (*puzzled*) Sorry?

Doris The garden. Just after the war. Looked after it for the rest of his life, too, but there hasn't been a soul bothered with it since he died. Shame, really. I hate to see a garden going to ruin for want of a helping hand.

Katherine I know. But it's so difficult, isn't it? It's obviously too much for Miss Bishop to look after, and with being so far from the village—well— what can she do?

Doris If I'd got *her* money, dear, I know what *I*'d do. I'd have a full-time gardener brought in and one or two servants to run the place. I mean, it's all very well wanting peace and quiet, but when one gets to her age, it's not safe to be on your own. What would have happened if her phone had been out of order? She could have been dead on the floor and we wouldn't have known about it for days.

Katherine Luckily it didn't come to that. But I know what you mean. (*She sighs*) The trouble is, she does like her privacy. I'm not even sure she's happy about *my* being here. (*Quickly*) Not that she's said anything.

Doris (*surprised*) I should think she hasn't. If it hadn't been for you offering to look after her for a while, she'd still have been stuck in Bellingford Hospital with no privacy at all. She should be downright grateful.

Katherine Oh, I'm sure she *is*, Mrs Meacham. I didn't mean to give you the wrong impression. It's just that after living alone for so long—well—the idea of having someone else in the house must be a bit unsettling for her.

Doris I don't see why. Unless she's worried you might be a spy for Mills and Boon trying to get a look at her latest book before she can get it to her publishers.

Katherine (*laughing*) There's not much fear of that. I'm more for *Death by the Dozen* than *Love Conquers All*. To tell you the truth, I've never read any of her books—though Mum was a great fan. I gave stacks of them to the church jumble sale after she died.

Doris (*in mock horror*) Katherine Willis. I don't know how you had the nerve. Hanbury's only claim to fame, and you giving her books to a jumble sale. (*She smiles*) Between you and me, they're a load of old rubbish, but I must say she's made her money out of them. Just goes to show there's still a place for romance even in this day and age. (*She rises*) Oh, well. I'd better be off. Thanks for the tea.

The door R opens, and Dr Andrew Thorne enters. He is a handsome man in his forties, charming and well dressed. He carries a doctor's bag or case

Andrew (*smiling*) I thought I recognized the voice. (*He puts his case on top of the chest of drawers*) Morning, Doris.

Doris (*returning the smile*) Morning, Doctor. How is she?

Andrew Oh, as well as can be expected. Give her a few more weeks and we'll see how she gets on. Can't hurry nature, you know. And how's young Brian? Any news from him, yet?

Doris About the baby, you mean? No. They're still waiting. It's a week overdue, now. Strikes me you modern doctors haven't progressed much in the past fifty years in spite of your modern technology. You just pick a date and hope for the best, don't you? Come on. Admit it. My old grandmother knew to the *hour* when one of the village girls was going to have a baby. And nine times out of ten, she could even tell you who the father was going to be.

They all laugh

Well. I'm on my way. See you next week. (*She rises*)

Doris exits cheerily. We see her pass the window L

Andrew (*amused*) Quite a character, our Doris.

Katherine (*moving up to the door to wave her off*) Yes.

Doris (*off*) Bye, Michael.

Andrew I ... er ... I wonder if I might have a word with you, Katherine. About Miss Bishop.

Katherine (*turning to him*) Yes?

Andrew (*awkwardly*) I'm not sure how to put this, but—well—I know I asked you to help out for a week or two—just till she was able to fend for herself again ... but ... the ... er ... the situation seems to have changed somewhat.

Katherine (*nodding*) You mean ... she'd like me to leave? Is that it?

Andrew gives her a puzzled look. There is the sound of a car, off, starting up and moving away

(*Quickly*) Oh it's all right. I'm not offended or anything. (*She smiles wryly*) I'd a feeling that things might not work out.

Andrew (*leading her to the settee*) What on earth are you talking about? Of course she doesn't want you to leave. Quite the opposite. She's absolutely delighted with you. As a matter of fact, she's just spent the last half-hour singing your praises. Sit down.

They sit on the settee

No. It ... er ... it's more of a *medical* problem I'm afraid. Putting it bluntly, her heart's not the only cause for concern. (*A slight pause*) I had a letter this morning. From Bellingford General. They ran a series of tests on her whilst she was in there. The results aren't good. They've given her eight to ten weeks.

Katherine (*stunned*) Oh, no! (*Bewildered*) But you just told Mrs Meacham ...

Andrew (*nodding*) I know. I ... er ... I didn't want *this* particular piece of gossip circulating round the village. The last thing she needs now is a string of visitors. (*He rises*) What she must have is rest—and as much of it as possible. Not a vestige of excitement. (*He moves down* R)

Katherine (*absorbing the news*) I see. (*Hesitantly*) What is it? If you don't mind my asking. Cancer?

Andrew Putting it in layman's terms—yes. But mercifully one of the kinder types. She'll have little or no pain. Just fade away gradually until the end.

Katherine (*softly*) How awful. She'll be going back to Bellingford, then?

Andrew (*shaking his head*) There wouldn't be much point. There's nothing they can do for her. (*Wryly*) Besides—even if I could arrange it, she'd never agree. Hospitals terrify her. She couldn't wait to get out this time.

Katherine (*after a slight pause*) How did she take it? The news, I mean.

Andrew I haven't told her. To be frank, she's got enough on her plate trying to cope with the heart condition. If she knew how little time she really has ...

Katherine (*quietly*) Yes. Yes. I see.

Andrew (*facing her*) That's really what I wanted to speak to you about. The time element. Obviously I'd like you to stay on, but is it going to be convenient? There is Michael to think about, isn't there?

Katherine (*nodding*) Yes. (*Slight pause*) I don't know, Doctor. I'd like to say yes, but—well—a few weeks is one thing ... three months ...

Andrew It could be less.

Katherine (*helplessly*) I don't know. I'd arranged to take Michael to Scotland. To my cousin's. Her youngest daughter's getting married on the seventeenth. (*Reluctantly*) I could always call her, I suppose ...

Andrew (*quickly*) No, no. Of course not. There's no need for that. You go ahead. Take him. It'll do you both good to get away for a while. I can arrange for someone to come in without any problem. Honestly, I can.

Katherine (*relieved*) If you're sure. (*Suddenly*) I could stay on till the sixteenth if that's any help?

Andrew (*smiling*) That'd be fine. Gives me plenty of time to set the wheels in motion. There's a firm in London with quite a decent reputation. I've used them once or twice in the past. I'll give them a call this afternoon. Sorry to have sprung this on you, Katherine, but it's just one of those things. If I'd known earlier ...

Katherine (*smiling*) Oh, that's all right, Doctor. It's what's best for Miss Bishop that matters, isn't it? (*Pause*) I suppose you'll have to contact her relatives now?

Andrew (*shaking his head*) Luckily there's no need. She doesn't have any. Poor old soul's the last of her line. (*He moves to pick up his case*)

Katherine (*quickly*) Oh, no. There *is* a nephew. I do know that.

Andrew (*halting in his tracks*) Nephew? (*He looks back at her*) Are you sure?

Katherine Well, yes. She mentioned him only this morning. Raymond Shipley ... or Shapley, I think she called him.

Andrew (*frowning*) Shapley?

Katherine Something like that.

Andrew (*giving a quick smile*) How extraordinary. I've been her doctor for the past twelve years and she's never mentioned any living relative, let alone a nephew. How did the subject arise?

Katherine With this morning's mail. I took everything into her as usual and she went through them over breakfast. Most of it was fan mail, but one letter was marked personal and private so I gave it to her while I was sorting out the others. It seemed to upset her a little and I asked if anything was wrong. She told me it was nothing. Just her nephew asking about her health. Then she laughed and said it'd been a long time since Raymond Shipley, or Shapley, had worried about her health.

Andrew (*frowning*) I can't understand it. I was convinced she was all alone in the world. (*Wryly*) Well, one lives and learns, doesn't one? Perhaps I'd better check it out with her? Find out for certain.

Katherine (*anxiously*) Oh, I'd rather you didn't. I mean—not straight out. I'd hate her to think I'd been gossiping.

Andrew (*reassuringly*) You needn't worry. I'll pretend I'd forgotten. You know how notorious my little "lapses of memory" are in the village? Between you and me, it's a carefully cultivated habit. Keeps me out of all kinds of trouble. (*He smiles*)

Katherine gives a relieved smile, then a slight frown

Katherine If he really *is* her nephew, he's going to be a very rich man, isn't he? She must be worth millions.

Andrew (*amused*) I don't think she's quite *that* rich. The tax man will have seen to that. But he's certainly going to inherit a tidy sum. Always assuming, of course, she's intending to leave it to him.

Katherine Who else would she leave it to?

Andrew (*shrugging*) Charity? The local cats' home? Who knows? She might even leave it to *me*. (*He laughs*)

Katherine (*wistfully*) It must be marvellous to be rich.

Andrew I suppose so. But being rich can also create problems. I shouldn't think it's all champagne and cav——

An anguished cry is heard, off R. *Andrew and Katherine look towards the window* R *to see a stumbling figure pass by*

Katherine (*alarmed*) Michael. (*She rises*)

Michael Willis stumbles into the porch and enters the room. He is about twenty years old, strikingly handsome, but an unfortunate accident of birth has given him a very limited mental ability. He is slow-moving, and his speech is almost non-existent. He communicates with difficulty through a range of sounds. He wears a pair of old, but clean jeans and comfortable trainer shoes. He is clutching at his right arm and blood streams from between his fingers. He is also smeared with blood down the right-hand side of his chest

(*Horrified*) Michael! (*She hurries to him*) What's happened? What have you done?

Michael wails oddly as she catches hold of him

Andrew (*briskly*) Let me see. (*He eases her aside quickly and tries to examine Michael's arm. Sharply*) Let go, Michael. Take your hand away.

Michael moans again and tries to twist away

(*More firmly*) Michael.
Katherine It's all right, Michael. It's all right. Let Doctor see.

Michael releases his arm and sobbing loudly buries his head into Katherine's shoulder. Andrew quickly examines Michael's arm

(*Soothingly*) Shhh. Shhh. (*She strokes his head*)
Andrew (*shaking his head*) Pretty nasty. Almost down to the bone. I'll need to get him to the surgery.
Katherine (*flustered and upset*) I'll tell Miss Bishop. (*She attempts to break free of Michael*)
Andrew No, no. There's no need for you to come. I'll see to him.
Katherine (*uncertainly*) I'm not sure . . . (*She glances at Michael*)
Andrew It's all right. He's in good hands.
Katherine (*quickly*) It's not that. It's just that . . . well . . . (*To Michael*) You go with Dr Thorne, Michael. Down to the surgery. He'll look after you. Make your arm better.
Andrew (*to Michael*) Slip you a few stiches in, eh? Won't take long.
Katherine (*to Michael*) I'll stay here.

Michael gives a wail and fights to free himself from Andrew's grip

(*Anxiously*) Michael. No. No.

Michael wails louder, clinging tightly to Katherine

It's all right, Michael. It's all right. Shh. Shh. (*She comforts him*)

Andrew crosses to his case and extracts a tourniquet. He wraps it round Michael's arm and tightens it. Michael moans

Andrew That should hold it for a while. (*To Katherine*) Looks like you'd better come with us after all.
Katherine (*apologetically*) I thought there might be a problem. (*To Michael*) It's all right. I'm coming with you. Don't cry. (*She gently eases herself free*) I'll just tell Miss Bishop. (*She heads for the door* R)
Andrew (*calling after her*) See if you can borrow a towel or something, too. Nothing grand.
Katherine (*nodding*) I'll be back in a minute.

She exits

Andrew (*examining the arm again*) Tch, tch, tch. Given yourself a right old war wound, haven't you? What were you doing, eh? Spot of bayonet practice. Made a real mess of yourself. (*He touches the gash gingerly*)

Michael ignores him, anxiously watching the door R

Good job you've had your tetanus jab, isn't it? Stop all those nasty germs having a go at you. Never mind. We'll soon have you fixed up. (*He glances around*) What have you done with your shirt?

Katherine hurries back into the room. She has removed her apron and carries a towel

Katherine (*breathlessly*) This is the best I can do. I've told Miss Bishop. She'll be fine for an hour or so and she's got the telephone in case there's a call.

Andrew Right. (*To Michael*) Come on, Jack the Ripper. Let's get you into the car. (*To Katherine as he takes the towel from her*) I should bring his shirt along, too. He'll be needing it when I've got him sewn up. (*He shepherds Michael towards the porch*)

Katherine It's probably down by the summer-house.

They exit and the front door closes behind them. We see Andrew and Michael pass the window L, *and Katherine the window* R. *A few moments later, she hurries back, clutching a shirt*

Car doors slam, off, and the car moves away

After a pause, we see the figure of a man passing the window R. *A moment later the front door opens cautiously and Raymond Shapley steps into the room. He is about thirty-five, good-looking, but sulky in character, though capable of superficial charm. He wears slacks, a summer shirt open at the neck and carries a light jacket over his arm. Silently he surveys the room; then, tossing his jacket over the back of the settee, he moves to the chest of drawers and examines its contents. Disappointed, he crosses to the Welsh dresser and does the same searching. Disappointed again, he utters a soft curse and turns to survey the room again. The objects on the mantelpiece attract his eye and he crosses to the fireplace to examine them. Selecting one that looks interesting, he takes hold of it and examines it, unaware that the door* R *is opening behind him*

Raymond (*with a satisfied smile*) Might be worth a pound or two in the right hands.

Marion Bishop, a frail woman of seventy-one, enters R. *She is wearing a dressing-gown over her night clothes, a mass of white hair framing her pale face. Her lips have a slight tinge of blue to them and she wears no make-up. She leans heavily on a stick*

Marion I very much doubt it. It's a reproduction. Mass-produced, I shouldn't wonder.

Raymond (*turning sharply; attempting pleasantry*) Aunt Marion. How nice to see you.

Marion (*coldly*) I wish I could say the same. Would you mind replacing that, Raymond. It may be worthless but it does have sentimental value.

Raymond Oh, yes. Yes. Of course. (*He replaces the object on the mantel-piece*)

Marion (*moving to the settee*) And to what do I owe the pleasure of this visit? Anticipation of my funeral, perhaps?

Raymond (*grinning*) Dear Aunt Marion. Still as suspicious as ever.

Marion (*drily*) And, in your case, with good reason. What are you doing here? What do you want?

Raymond Having trouble with your mail deliveries? I sent you a letter.

Marion Oh, yes. I filed it where it belonged. In the waste-paper basket. (*She sits*) Who told you I was ill?

Raymond (*moving behind her*) Don't tell me you've forgotten how famous you are, Auntie dear? It was in the paper. About a week after I came out. They gave me time off for good behaviour. Kind of them, wasn't it? (*Easily*) I was "dining out" near King's Cross station and spotted it in the gossip column. (*He leans over the settee back*) Ever thought of doing that, Auntie dear? Eating fish and chips from an old newspaper and huddling under a bridge to shelter from the rain?

Marion (*coldly*) If you're expecting sympathy, you've come to the wrong person. You made your bed over twenty years ago. Don't come crying to me to change your sheets.

Raymond (*smiling*) Bravo. Spoken like a true queen of romance. You're getting better in your old age. That last bit was quite poetical.

Marion (*patiently*) I assume you do have a reason for coming here? In which case I'd appreciate you getting down to brass tacks and then leaving. I'd prefer you not to be here when Miss Willis arrives back.

Raymond She the piece who's just left?

Marion (*frowning*) You've seen her?

Raymond I wouldn't have mentioned it if I hadn't, would I? Been watching the place for the past two hours. From inside the summer-house. Waiting for a chance to get you alone. What's the deal with young nature boy? Bit of a nutcase, is he? Few screws missing in the top storey?

Marion (*frostily*) If you mean is he retarded, then the answer is yes. His mother was involved in an accident shortly before his birth. He is, however, more of a human being than you'll ever be. At least he's willing to work for his money.

Raymond (*moving R; with a smile*) Still can't resist it, can you? Have to get your little digs in. (*Sourly*) God. You're so predictable, it hurts.

Marion Unfortunately, not enough.

Raymond (*easily*) I saw the whole thing, you know. He was perched up in one of the trees, chopping at the ivy, and missed his footing. The garden shears were under him when he hit the ground. (*He grins*) I was expecting him to scream blue murder and let rip a bit, but he just sort of staggered to his feet and started blubbering like a baby. That's when I realized he must be a bit cracked and made myself scarce. I didn't want anyone coming out and finding me down there, so I shinned over the wall and into the lane. Could have saved myself the trouble, couldn't I?

Marion You could have saved everyone trouble by keeping away completely. I've told you before—you're not welcome here.

Raymond (*nodding*) Oh, yes. Every time I've contacted you. I keep forgetting. Have to protect the old image, haven't we? Mustn't let the locals know there's a skeleton in the cupboard. "Baa, baa, black sheep". (*He smiles savagely*) Well that's just too bad, Auntie dear, because here I am, and here I'm going to stay until I get what I came for. And we both know what that is, don't we?

Marion We've already discussed the matter on several occasions, Raymond, and I've no intention of discussing it again. If that's all you came for, you may as well return to London now. This very minute.

Raymond (*harshly*) It's *my* money. It was left to me.

Marion (*firmly*) In my safekeeping.

Raymond (*loudly*) But it's *mine*, you old bitch, it's *mine*. Are you deaf as well as senile? Can't you hear me?

Marion (*calmly*) It would be difficult not to, in your present state. Kindly stop behaving like an hysterical schoolgirl and lower your voice.

Raymond (*savagely*) Yes, ma'am, no, ma'am, three bags full, ma'am. (*With quiet menace*) You're holding on to three hundred and fifty thousand pounds of *my* money. Money my mother intended me to have. Now hand it over nicely or I may have to do something you won't be very pleased about.

Marion (*amused*) And what's so unusual in that? You haven't done much that's pleased me since you were a boy in short trousers. (*Scornfully*) Look at you. A fully-grown man who's never done an honest day's work in his life. How your father would have loved you. Two peas from a single pod. Twin blemishes on the face of humanity.

Raymond (*nodding with satisfaction*) Oh, yes. I thought you'd have to drag him into it. What's it going to be this time? The shortened version, or the full drama of how he deserted his dying wife to run off with a cheap little floozie from Birmingham and kill himself in a drunken car smash? Would you like me to start it off for you? I know it all by heart.

Marion I'm quite sure you do. If nothing else you've ever learned stays inside that twisted brain of yours, at least I've made quite certain you know the truth about him. (*Tiredly*) Now please go away. I haven't the energy to cope with you any longer. I need rest.

Raymond (*laughing unpleasantly*) Oh, I'm afraid you won't be getting much of that, Auntie dear. Not after I've taken my story to the press. You'll have reporters crawling round here like ants.

Marion Press?

Raymond (*nodding*) The *Sun. Daily Mirror. News of the World*. All those nasty newspapers that only disreputable people read. I can almost see the headlines now. "Queen of romance cheats jailbird nephew out of inheritance. Marion Bishop in cash fiddle".

Marion (*tartly*) Don't be so ridiculous.

Raymond What's ridiculous about it? I'm sure your devoted readers would be only too fascinated to hear how you've been enjoying yourself with my money whilst keeping me firmly tucked away out of sight. How much of it's left, I wonder?

Marion (*coldly*) More than you could ever imagine. And the sooner you realize that the world doesn't owe you a living and settle down to doing an honest day's work for an honest day's pay, you'll discover how rich you really are.

Raymond (*sneering*) In the spiritual sense, of course.

Marion No. In the material sense. (*Quietly*) I'd no intention of telling you this at the moment, but it's perfectly obvious that unless you're given some sort of incentive, you'll spend the rest of your life in a state of impoverishment or in prison. At the present moment you are worth somewhere in the region of six hundred thousand pounds. And that is apart from anything I might decide to leave you when I die.

Raymond (*stunned*) Six hundred thousand? (*Suspiciously*) How come?

Marion Fortunately for you, I have the intelligence to use the brain God gave me. I took financial advice on how best to make your money work for you. Some I invested, and the rest was used to set up a trust fund. Both have reaped excellent dividends. You're a wealthy young man, Raymond, and could be even more so providing you smarten up your ideas.

Raymond And if I don't?

Marion Then it's your loss. Naturally you'll receive your own money on my death, but you won't see a penny of mine. I'll make quite certain of that.

Raymond I'll do a deal with you.

Marion No. No deals. I've told you before. Your mother left that money with me because she knew you couldn't be trusted with it. Six months after her death, you wouldn't have a penny left. It would all have been spent on fast cars and riotous living.

Raymond What difference——

Marion Difficult though it may be for you to believe, your mother loved you very much. She wanted you to enjoy the good things of life—the things that a steady job and a healthy bank account could give you. But equally so, she was not prepared to finance a way of life that was total anathema to her.

Raymond (*sourly*) It wouldn't have been a way of life if she'd loosened up on the purse strings a few years earlier.

Marion (*tiredly*) Raymond. Raymond. Who are you trying to fool? Money was never a problem for you. If anything you were given too much of it. You had the opportunity to better yourself, but instead, you've spent almost half your life in custody on one charge or another. No, Raymond. Before I release that money to you, you have to knuckle down and prove to me that the leopard really has changed his spots. Do I make myself clear?

Raymond But I need that money, damn you. I need it.

Marion (*rising*) I'm sorry. That's my last word on the matter. You can see yourself out, can't you? (*She moves towards the door* R)

Raymond (*grabbing her arm*) Wait.

Marion (*icily*) Let go of my arm. (*She tries to pull free*)

Raymond Listen to me.

Marion (*struggling*) Let go.

Raymond (*pleading*) Just ten thousand.

Marion No.

She tugs furiously to free herself, but Raymond hangs on. For a moment there is a silent struggle, then Marion's eyes open wide and she gives a loud gasp. Startled, he gapes at her as she sags in his arms, eyes closing

Raymond (*gasping*) Aunt Marion?

There is no answer

(*Panic-stricken*) Aunt Marion?

He drags her to the settee with an effort and lowers her on to it. She flops there lifelessly

(*Louder*) Aunt Marion? (*Desperately he looks round the room. Quickly crossing to the chest, he flicks through the address book, then finding the number he wants, picks up the telephone and begins to dial. Suddenly he pauses as an idea flashes into his mind. A slow smile crosses his face, and he replaces the receiver. Taking a handkerchief from his pocket, he carefully wipes his fingerprints off the phone and the address book, then replaces the handkerchief in his pocket. Moving back to the settee, he picks up his coat, drapes it over his arm, moves to the front door and looks back*) Bye-bye, Aunt Marion. It was nice knowing you. (*He laughs nastily*)

He exits. A moment later we see him pass the window L

Black-out

SCENE 2

The same. Two weeks later

Little has been changed in the past two weeks. The groceries' box has been removed and the flowers replaced. The tea things have been cleared away and a different book is by the table lamp

The room is rather gloomy as torrential rain is falling and low rolls of thunder can be heard. The fire is lit and the table lamp throws a soft pool of light

Doris Meacham is sitting on the settee drinking coffee and chatting to Katherine who sits beside her. Katherine is only half listening, seeming rather uneasy; her drink is untouched on the coffee table

Doris (*sipping at her coffee*) You could have knocked me down with a feather when I heard about it. I just couldn't take it in. I mean—it all happened so quickly, didn't it? (*She shrugs*) Mind you, if you've got to go, I suppose it's the best way. We're going to miss her in the village, though. Very well liked she was.

Katherine (*absently*) Yes.

Doris (*thoughtfully*) I wonder what'll happen to the house and things? (*Wryly*) Probably go to charity with her having no family, eh? Don't you think so?

Katherine (*still far away*) Yes. Yes. I expect so.

Doris (*smiling*) You haven't been listening to a word I've said, have you?
Katherine (*guilty*) Yes. Yes. Of course I have.

Doris looks at her steadily

(*Shamefaced*) No. (*She sighs*) I'm sorry, Mrs Meacham. To be honest I
was thinking about Michael. I'm a bit worried about him.
Doris (*concerned*) Why's that, dear? He's not ill or anything, is he?
Katherine (*quickly*) Oh, no. No. Nothing like that. It's just that he's all
alone in the house and—well—he's not too happy about thunder. If it
gets any worse, he might panic because I'm not there.
Doris (*relieved*) Oh, well. If that's all it is, you needn't fret yourself. I'll call
in on my way back and take him down to the shop with me. He can have
lunch with us and help feed the chickens. He'd like that, wouldn't he? He
knows he'll be safe with us.
Katherine Oh, thank you, Mrs Meacham. It'd be a big weight off my mind.
I'd never have left him, but I thought they'd have been here ages ago, and
it was so nice first thing. Thank goodness I packed the cases before I came
out.
Doris Yes. You're away this afternoon, aren't you? I only hope the
weather's better in Scotland than it is down here.
Katherine Me too. It'll be awful if it rains on her wedding-day.
Doris We had three inches of snow on ours. Talk about getting cold feet at
the last minute. (*She chuckles*) Well, I'd best be off. (*She rises*) Thanks for
the coffee, and don't worry about Michael. We'll look after him till you
arrive.

Katherine sees Doris to the front door

I'd still like to know about the house though. It's exactly the sort of thing
our Brian and Stephanie are looking for. Now they've got Sharon they'll
be needing a bigger place. A flat's no good for bringing up children, is it?
They haven't even a garden she could play in. Besides, it'd be nice having
them live a bit closer.

There is a great crash of thunder

(*Briskly*) Don't worry. I'll be there in five minutes. (*She exits into the
porch and takes her raincoat from a hook*) See you later. (*She looks out*)
Oh. It looks like they're here. There's a car turning in.

Katherine goes to the porch to look

Katherine (*concerned*) They're going to get soaked. (*She fumbles in the
umbrella stand for an umbrella*)
Doris (*taking the umbrella from her*) Here, let me. No point in everybody
getting wet.

She opens the umbrella and dashes out

(*Off; calling*) Stay where you are. I'm coming.

*After a short pause, Laura Vinnecombe hurries past the window L, holding
the umbrella. She enters the porch. She is an attractive thirty-six years old,*

slim and well dressed. She wears a wig in contrasting colour to her own hair, and a light coat, spattered with rain. She appears a cold person, rarely smiling except when she feels it is expected of her. One feels she is not altogether a person to make a friend of, but she is capable and efficient

Katherine (*warmly*) Isn't it terrible? (*She takes the umbrella*) Do go in. I've got the fire lit.

Laura enters the room. Katherine shakes the rain off the umbrella as:

Andrew stumbles into the porch with two suitcases

Andrew (*dropping the cases*) What a day. (*He shakes himself*)
Katherine Dreadful.
Andrew Hardly see a thing through the windscreen.
Katherine Go through, Doctor. I'll see to the cases. (*She puts the umbrella back into the stand*)

Andrew enters the room. Laura gives him a nervous smile; he winks at her reassuringly

Andrew (*moving to her*) Come on. Make yourself at home.

He helps her off with her coat and drapes it on the chair by the window. Katherine brings in the cases and closes the door

Katherine I'll just leave them here for the minute. (*She crosses to Laura with a smile and holds out her hand*) Katherine Willis.
Laura Hello. (*She shakes hands with Katherine*)
Katherine Welcome to Moor View.
Andrew (*amused*) Not much of a view at the minute. Just look at it coming down. (*He gazes out of the window*)
Katherine (*warmly*) Do sit down. Warm yourselves up in front of the fire. I'll go put more coffee on—or would you prefer tea?
Laura Tea for me, if you don't mind. (*She sits on the settee*)
Andrew Fine by me.
Katherine Won't take more than a few minutes. (*She begins to exit, then halts*) Oh. (*She turns back*) Do you take sugar, Nurse Ledston?

Laura throws a startled look at Andrew

Andrew (*slapping the side of his head with the flat of his hand*) Blast. I knew there was something I had to tell you. This ... er ... this *isn't* Nurse Ledston. It's Nurse Vinnecombe. Laura Vinnecombe.
Katherine (*surprised*) Oh.
Andrew Nurse Ledston couldn't make it, after all. She ... er ... had to go out on another job. Laura's come down as a substitute. (*He smiles*) I meant to tell you on Wednesday, but it completely slipped my mind with Mrs Carfax dying. (*To Laura*) Old lady living alone in the village. Died sometime Saturday night, and wasn't found till Tuesday.
Katherine We were just talking about her. Before you arrived. Doris was wondering if the house might be suitable for Brian and his wife.

Andrew (*shaking his head*) Shouldn't think so. Way out of their price range. Unless, of course, Doris and Ken are thinking of helping out. But getting back to Laura, here. I should have told you. It's my fault, entirely.

Katherine (*slightly embarrassed*) It's nobody's fault. I'm just thankful somebody came. (*To Laura*) It must have been an awful rush for you to arrange everything at such short notice.

Laura (*forcing a smile*) Not really. I'm quite used to it by now. I keep a suitcase packed behind the front door.

Katherine (*smiling*) Sensible move. I'll get that tea.

Katherine exits R

Laura (*anxiously*) Andrew . . .

Andrew (*softly*) It's all right. There's nothing to worry about.

Laura But what if she starts asking questions?

Andrew She won't. (*He sits beside her*) I've already told you. She's going away this afternoon and won't be back for at least a week. If we stick to the story we've agreed on, it'll be all plain sailing.

Laura (*after a pause*) And you're sure there'll be no problem with Miss Bishop?

Andrew Nothing you can't handle. It's only a fortnight since her last attack and she's weak as a kitten. Providing things go as planned, I'll have you out of England by the end of next month. The important thing is not to rush things. We don't want to make any slips. Understand?

Laura (*irritated*) I'm not a complete idiot.

Andrew Nobody's saying you are. (*He takes her hand*) I'm sorry Laura. It's just that we've got to keep you out of sight for a while. They'll never think of looking for you here, not in a million years. And even if they did, you've got nothing to worry about. At the present moment you don't fit any description they've got. Now just relax and let's take things one step at a time. All right?

There is a great crash of thunder

Sounds like it's getting worse.

Laura I didn't think it could. (*Pause*) What about tonight? I mean—you will be here, won't you? You *are* coming back?

Andrew Do you want me to?

Laura (*nodding*) If you can.

Andrew (*reassuringly*) No problem. I'll make it as soon as it gets dark. Think you can knock a meal together?

Laura I can try. It's been a long time.

Andrew I'll raid the wine cellar.

Katherine enters with a tray of tea things

Katherine Here we are.

Andrew quickly releases Laura's hand

Feeling any warmer? (*She crosses to the coffee table and deposits the tray*)

Laura Oh, much. Thank you.

Andrew Fine.
Katherine Help yourselves, do.
Laura Thank you. (*She begins to pour the tea*)
Andrew (*to Katherine*) You're not joining us?
Katherine (*smiling*) No. I'd better be on my way. There's still a few bits and pieces to pack.
Andrew You're not walking back in this lot. You'll be drowned before you get to the road. Hang on a minute and I'll run you into the village.
Katherine No, no. It's all right. I've got my mac and I can borrow the umbrella.
Andrew (*standing*) I wouldn't hear of it. We can't expect you to come out here to get things ready, then send you out into the storm like little Orphan Annie. And besides—if the car breaks down, you can always get out and help me push.
Katherine Well, if you really don't mind?
Andrew Consider it settled. I'll just have my tea and we'll be on our way.

Laura hands him a cup

Thanks.
Katherine (*to Laura*) I ... er ... I'll take your cases up, then. I thought you might like the room next to Miss Bishop. It overlooks the garden and there's a connecting door if you have to go to her during the night. The bathroom and toilet are just along the corridor.
Laura Thank you.

Katherine picks up the cases and exits R

(*Sipping her tea*) Nice girl.
Andrew Yes. Very.
Laura (*watching him covertly*) Married?
Andrew No. Why?
Laura Nothing. I just wondered. (*She rises and moves down R, sipping at her tea. There is a silence, then she turns back to face him*) Andrew?
Andrew (*looking up*) Yes?
Laura If they do manage to trace me here ...
Andrew They won't. I've promised you.
Laura But if they do ...
Andrew There's not a snowball in hell's chance. You've got a new identity, you've changed your appearance, and you're a hundred and fifty miles away from the last place you were seen. How could you be traced?
Laura I don't know. It's just that I've got this strange feeling.
Andrew (*rising, crossing to her*) Laura ...

There is a tremendous crash of thunder

The front door flies open and Michael Willis stumbles into the room. He is wearing a sleeveless jumper, cream shirt and dark trousers. He is soaking wet and his hair is plastered to his head. He is making frantic, unintelligible sounds

Laura (*stepping back; frightened*) No!

Andrew (*turning swiftly*) Michael. (*He grasps hold of Michael*) What on earth are *you* doing out here? Where's your coat, for God's sake?

Michael desperately tries to speak, sobbing and terrified

(*To Laura*) It's all right. It's Katherine's brother.
Michael Ka'rin. Ka'rin.
Andrew (*holding on to him*) Yes. She's here. She's here. Now calm down. There's nothing to be frightened of. Nothing's going to hurt you.
Laura Is he—all right?
Andrew Brain damaged, but quite harmless. Terrified of thunder. (*To Michael*) Come on. Over to the fire. There's a good lad.

Andrew leads Michael towards the fireplace

(*To Laura*) Close the door and give her a shout, would you? (*To Michael*) God in heaven, boy. You're like a drowned rat.

Michael continues moaning

Laura closes the front door and exits R

Michael Ka'rin.
Andrew (*nodding*) Yes. Yes. She's coming. With you in a minute. Just warm yourself up, eh? Stop you catching your death.
Laura (*off; calling*) Miss Willis? Katherine?
Michael Hunner. Hunner.
Andrew (*not understanding*) Yes. Yes. I'm sure it is. Now stay here while I find a towel or something. You're dripping all over the carpet.

There is another crash of thunder. Michael grabs hold of Andrew with a scream of fear

It's all right, lad. It's all right. (*He holds on to him tightly*)

Katherine hurriedly enters R, *followed by Laura*

Katherine (*dismayed*) Oh, Michael. (*She moves to him*)

Michael tears free of Andrew and flings himself into Katherine's arms, making incomprehensible sounds

Why didn't you stay where you were, love? You're soaking. Shhh.
Andrew I'll find a towel.

Andrew exits R

Katherine (*comforting Michael*) It's all right. It can't hurt you. Shhh. Shhh.
Laura (*awkwardly*) He just burst in here. Frightened the life out of me.
Katherine (*apologetically*) I am sorry. He must have come looking for me when the rain started. He's absolutely terrified of thunder. Always has been. (*To Michael*) Shhh. Shhh.

Andrew enters with a towel

Andrew Here we are. Let's get some of that water off you before you turn into a fish.

He hands the towel to Katherine who begins to mop away the excess water from Michael

Why didn't you put your raincoat on before you came out, eh? Have to get changed again, now, won't you?

Katherine I suppose he just panicked and ran out.

Andrew (*to Michael*) What's going to happen if you catch your death of cold, eh? It won't be a wedding you'll be going to. It'll be a funeral.

Katherine (*smiling*) He's not going to catch a cold, are you, Michael? That's an old wives' tale, isn't it?

Andrew Oh, I don't know. I bet there's nothing he'd like better than to be propped up in bed with a nice bunch of grapes and a pretty nurse to look after him. (*To Michael*) Eh, Michael? (*To Katherine*) How's that arm of his going on, by the way? All cleared up?

Katherine Oh, yes. It's still a bit red where the stitches were, but it's healing beautifully.

Andrew (*to Laura*) Gashed himself with a pair of garden shears, week before last. Lucky I was here when it happened.

Katherine (*to Michael*) Miss Vinnecombe's a nurse, Michael. She's come to look after Miss Bishop while we're away.

Michael shyly peers round Katherine at Laura

Andrew Well ... I'd better run you two back to the village. (*To Michael*) Get yourself into some dry clothes before you catch the train. And don't forget to bring me a bottle of whisky back, will you? The real stuff, mind. None of these Japanese imports.

The telephone rings

I'll get it. (*He crosses to the phone and answers*) Hanbury double five four nine three. ... Sorry? ... Oh, yes, Doris. Yes. She's here. Hang on. (*To Katherine*) It's for you. Doris Meacham.

Katherine It'll be about Michael, I expect.

She crosses to him, Michael holding on to her

(*On the phone*) Hello? ... Yes. Yes, Mrs Meacham. I know. He turned up here. ... No, no. He's quite safe. Wet through, of course, but—— ... No, no. I'm just sorry you—— ... (*She laughs*) No. Really. Doctor Thorne's running us back. ... Yes. Yes. I will. Of course. We'll see you later. We'll call in as we pass. ... Yes. Thank you. Bye. (*She replaces the receiver*) She found the door wide open and Michael missing. (*To Michael*) You made her feel quite worried, you know.

There is another crash of thunder. Michael quickly presses himself to Katherine

Andrew I'll open up the car. (*He fumbles for his keys*)

Katherine (*to Laura*) I'm sorry to have to leave you so soon. You were a bit later than I expected but I think you'll find everything.

Andrew exits into the porch, picks up an umbrella and hurries out

There's a week's supply of groceries and things in the kitchen and plenty of extras in the store cupboards—but if you do want any more, Mrs Meacham will always bring it over if you give her a call. The number's on the pad. The surgery number's on there too, if you need the doctor, and I've left a few other useful ones. You don't have to worry about breakfast—apart from your own, of course. She hasn't been eating anything except the odd slice of toast. It's mainly very weak tea, but she'll tell you herself, I'm sure.

Laura Don't worry. I'm sure I'll cope.

Katherine Yes. Well ... I suppose we'd better be off. (*To Michael*) Say goodbye to Nurse, Michael.

He makes no attempt to do so, but stares at her

Laura Have a nice time, then.

The car horn sounds, off

Katherine We'll do our best, won't we? (*She moves into the porch and gets her mackintosh*)

Michael remains standing, looking at Laura in close scrutiny. Laura stares back at him

Michael?

There is no reaction from Michael

Michael?

Still nothing. Frowning, Katherine re-enters the room and takes him by the arm

Michael?

Michael (*turning to Katherine as though emerging from a trance*) Haaaar. Haaaar. (*He turns to gaze at Laura again*)

Katherine looks puzzled, then realizes and gives an apologetic smile

Katherine (*to Laura*) Oh, I ... er ... I think he likes your hair.

Laura (*touching her wig*) What do you mean?

Katherine (*awkwardly*) It's the same style and colour as Mum's. She died some years ago, but he still remembers her, you see.

Laura (*relieved*) Oh ...

Katherine I'm sorry if he embarrassed you.

Laura That's—all right. (*She forces a smile*)

The car horn sounds again, off

Katherine Come along, Michael. Doctor's waiting.

She leads him out into the porch, opens the umbrella and gives it to him

(*To Laura*) Bye.

Katherine and Michael exit

After a few moments, Laura closes the front door, goes to the settee and sits

There is the sound of a car off, moving away and a crash of thunder

Laura removes her wig, shakes her own hair, then rises and moves aimlessly down R. Suddenly she comes to a decision, she goes to the telephone, lifts the receiver and dials a nine-digit number. She impatiently waits for an answer

Laura (*on the phone*) Hello? Is that you Chris? ... It's Laura. Laura Sanderson.

There is another great crash of thunder

Black-out

SCENE 3

The same. Ten days later. Afternoon

The sun is shining and the room is empty. The vase of flowers has been changed for fresh ones, and the tea things, towel, and Laura's coat have been removed. A portable radio is on the coffee table and an announcer is speaking

Announcer ... and the strike, which is now entering its eighth week, seems likely to continue through October. (*Pause*) British Rail today announced that fares would rise again on November the third. This will be the second increase this year and the news provoked angry reactions from commuters. Mr Steven Lister, Chairman of RUPTA, the Rail Users and Public Transport Association, immediately accused British Rail of blatant profiteering, but a spokesman for the company denied this, saying that the increases were necessary if present standards were to be maintained.

Marion enters from the door R. She is much paler than before and moves with an effort. She carries a small tray on which is a teapot, milk-jug, cup and saucer and a spoon. She crosses to the coffee table

However, Mr Lister was plainly unconvinced and stated that a letter of protest would be sent to the Prime Minister. (*Pause*) The body of the middle-aged woman found yesterday by schoolchildren on a nature walk, near Camberley, Surrey, has been identified.

Marion puts the tray down and begins to pour herself a cup of tea. As she does so, the telephone begins to ring

She is Doris Benwood Ledston, a forty-six year-old private nurse who vanished after leaving her London home nine days ago. The naked body was discovered in thick shrubbery as——

Marion turns off the radio and moves towards the phone

Marion (*muttering*) All right. All right. I'm coming. (*She picks up the receiver*) Hanbury five five four nine three. ... Five five four nine three.

... Hello? Hello? Is anyone there? Hello? (*With a vexed frown she replaces the receiver and heads back towards the coffee table*)

The telephone rings again. With a look of annoyance, she returns to it and picks up the receiver

(*Sharply*) Hanbury double five four nine three. . . . (*Surprised*) Oh, (*she gives a little laugh*) Dr Thorne. . . . No, no, no. I thought it was my anonymous admirer again. . . . My anonymous admirer . . . Well, that's what I call him—or her. . . . I beg your pardon? I didn't quite . . . Oh, no, no. Never says anything. Not even the traditional heavy breathing. (*She laughs*) . . . I'm sorry? . . . No, no. Of course not. I may write romantic novels, Doctor, but I'm a tough old bird. It'll take more than anonymous phone calls to frighten me. . . . Good heavens, no. I wouldn't dream of it. Besides, Nurse Vinnecombe's taking very good care of me. . . .

During the following Laura passes the window R, *and a moment later enters from the front door. She wears her uniform and carries a small bunch of fresh cut flowers and a small pair of scissors*

Yes. Yes. She's in the garden. If you'll just hold on I'll——(*She sees Laura enter*) Oh. Here she is now. (*To Laura*) Dr Thorne. He'd like a word with you. (*She holds out the receiver*)

Laura Thank you. (*She puts down the flowers and scissors and takes it*) Hello? . . .

Marion goes back to the settee, settles herself and drinks tea

No. Just picking a few flowers. . . . Yes. Yes. . . . Well, I'm not sure. Could I call you back? . . . Oh. Yes. That might be better. . . . Yes. Yes. We'll expect you shortly, then. . . . Yes. Thank you. (*She replaces the receiver and turns to Marion*) He's coming out to us. Should be here in about fifteen minutes.

Marion Oh? For any particular reason?

Laura Something's cropped up for tomorrow, so he'd like to give you your check-up this afternoon instead of in the morning. That is all right, isn't it?

Marion (*sighing deeply*) Yes, I suppose so. I wasn't planning on doing anything except perhaps going back to bed. I can't understand why I feel so tired all the time. I haven't half the energy I used to have.

Laura (*picking up the flowers*) I think we all suffer from that complaint, Miss Bishop, but in your case there's a perfectly reasonable answer to it. I'll put these in water. (*She moves to the door* R)

Marion I can't even settle to write, and that's almost unheard of. Even in my worst years I've managed at least two books.

Laura (*patiently*) You have been rather ill. It'll take you some time to get back to normal.

Marion (*protesting*) But I'm six months behind with *The Candle and the Moth*. The words just don't seem to flow.

Laura Perhaps it's "writer's block" or whatever they call it. I shouldn't worry. As soon as you start to pick up, it'll pass.
Marion (*shaking her head*) No, no. I've had "writer's block" many a time. This is nothing like it. It's more a kind of ... of ... mental lethargy.
Laura Well why not mention it to Dr Thorne when he arrives? Perhaps he can suggest something. (*She glances through the window* L) Hello. I think we have visitors.
Marion Who is it?
Laura Miss Willis and her brother, by the look of it. Yes. It is.
Marion (*pleased*) You'd better put the kettle on, Laura. I expect they'll be glad of a drink. And see if you can find a few biscuits for Michael. I think he likes the cream-filled kind, but bring what we have.
Laura Yes, Miss Bishop.

Laura exits R

Katherine and Michael pass the window L. *There is a knock on the door*

Marion (*calling*) Come in.

Katherine opens the door and enters. She is obviously delighted to see Marion. Michael carefully wipes his feet on the mat in the porch. He carries two small gift-wrapped packages

Welcome back, dear.
Katherine (*warmly*) Oh, Miss Bishop. You look marvellous. (*To Michael*) Come on.

Michael enters the room, smiling shyly

(*To Marion*) How are you feeling?
Marion Oh, as well as can be expected. Come in. Take your coats off. Let me have a look at you.

Katherine closes the door, slips off her coat and helps Michael off with his

Now then, Michael. Did you have a nice time in Scotland?

Michael grins broadly, nods his head and makes unintelligible sounds

Katherine Oh, we had a lovely time, thank you. The weather was gorgeous. We got lots of photographs and everything went off beautifully. I'll bring the snaps over and show you them when I've had them all developed. Some of us (*she indicates Michael*) even found time to buy a few presents. (*To Michael*) Come on, Michael. Where's the present you bought for Miss Bishop?

Michael beams and holds out a package to Marion

That's right.
Marion (*affecting great excitement*) Oh, I wonder what it is? (*She takes the gift*) Can I open it now?

Michael beams and nods, making sounds. Marion unwraps the package to reveal a small box of shortbread fingers

(*With great pleasure*) Real Scottish shortbread. My very favourite. Oh, thank you, Michael. Come here and let me give you a kiss.

Michael looks down at the floor

(*To Katherine*) There. I've gone and embarrassed him now.

Katherine and Marion laugh gently. Michael looks up and makes odd sounds, tugging at Katherine's sleeve

Katherine (*shaking her head at him*) No, I hadn't forgotten. (*To Marion*) He bought something for Nurse Vinnecombe, too. She seems to have made a big impression on him.
Marion (*smiling*) She's in the kitchen making fresh tea. I was just about to have mine when we saw you arriving, so we can all have a cup together. Sit down, dear. There's plenty of room.
Katherine (*sitting*) I wouldn't have bothered you today, but he was so excited I had to bring him over to give you your presents. I hope you don't mind?
Marion No, no. Of course not. I'm delighted to see you.
Katherine We've only just arrived home. Haven't even had time to unpack.
Marion You must tell me all about it. It's been years since I was in Scotland—nineteen-fifty-six or seven, I think. I was doing research on my Flora Macdonald book. Such a beautiful country. Where was it you were?
Katherine Oh, just outside Edinburgh. A little place called Ratho. It's only small, but it's very nice.
Marion And they both live there, do they? Your niece and her new husband.
Katherine (*quickly*) Oh no. Janet was born there, of course, but David's from Surrey. A few miles outside Camberley. They met at university.

Laura enters with a tray of tea things

Marion (*frowning*) Camberley. There was a nasty murder there the other day. Some poor nurse found strangled in the shrubbery.

Laura stops dead in her tracks. Michael thrusts the gift he is holding at her and she looks at it blankly before recovering herself and continuing to the coffee table. Michael follows her looking puzzled and hurt

(*Noticing her*) Ah, here we are. Do help yourself, dear.

Katherine greets Laura with a warm smile. Laura responds in an absent kind of way then turns to exit R

Laura (*as she does so*) I'll just get the biscuits. (*She collides with Michael*) Oh . . .
Katherine (*gently*) Careful, Michael. You nearly knocked Nurse over.

Michael thrusts the gift at Laura again, uttering sounds

(*To Laura*) Oh, he's brought you a little present back.

Laura (*uncomfortably*) Oh. Thank you. (*She forces a smile and takes the gift*)

Katherine He chose it all by himself, I hope you like it.

Laura (*awkwardly*) I'm—sure I will. (*To Michael*) It was very kind of you.

Laura hurries off

Michael looks after her, a little frown on his face

Katherine (*smiling*) It's all right. She'll be back in a minute. (*To Marion*) Sorry. A nurse, did you say? (*She picks up the teapot and begins to pour*)

Marion (*nodding*) Yes. It's terrible, isn't it? I don't know what the world is coming to. You hardly dare leave your own home these days. Robbery. Rape. Violence. I can't tell you how glad I am that my life's nearly over.

Katherine (*protesting*) Miss Bishop——

Marion (*shaking her head*) Oh, I'll be quite happy to go, dear. I was just saying to Laura, I haven't half the energy I used to have.

Katherine You have been rather ill. (*She hands a cup of tea to Michael*)

Marion That's exactly the answer she gave me.

Katherine Well, then. (*She sips at her tea*)

Laura enters with a small plate of assorted biscuits. She carries them to the coffee table

Laura No custard creams, I'm afraid, but there's quite a selection here. Did you have a nice time, Miss Willis?

Katherine (*warmly*) Lovely, thank you. We hadn't seen them in years, so we had a lot to catch up on.

Michael moves to Laura and touches her arm, making anxious sounds

(*Reprovingly*) Michael. (*To Laura, smiling*) Oh. I think he wants to know if you liked your present.

Laura (*blankly*) Present . . . ? Oh, yes. The present. (*She gives a quick smile*) I . . . er . . . haven't had time to open it yet. (*To Michael, brightly*) I'd better do it now, hadn't I?

Michael smiles and nods excitedly

I won't be a minute. I left it in the kitchen.

Laura exits. After a moment, Michael follows her out

Marion Bless him.

Katherine We thought about you a lot during the last ten days. I even called Dr Thorne once to ask how you were bearing up.

Marion Yes, he told me. But you shouldn't have bothered, dear.

Katherine I kept seeing you lying there—on the day we found you. Couldn't get it out of my mind. I'd never have forgiven myself if . . . well . . . if we hadn't arrived back when we did. I felt terrible about leaving you alone.

Marion (*firmly*) Now that's enough of that. We discussed all this at the hospital. What happened was nothing to do with you. It was my own fault for disobeying orders. I should have stayed in bed as I'd been told.

Anyway, it won't happen again. Nurse Vinnecombe will see to that. She fusses round me like a mother hen. (*She makes herself more comfortable*) By the way, were there any phone calls whilst I was in hospital? Apart from the ones you told me about, that is?

Katherine I don't think so. I made a note of every one I took.

Marion And there were no others?

Katherine Well, only the usual ones. Mrs Meacham for the grocery order. Dr Thorne. And the one from the butcher.

Marion No strange men or wrong numbers?

Katherine (*puzzled*) Not that I remember. Why? Is something wrong?

Marion No, no. It's just that ... well ... for the past few days I've been getting some rather odd calls.

Katherine (*concerned*) You mean—obscene ones?

Marion (*laughing*) No, no. Nothing like that. I don't think anyone would ring up an old biddy like me to practise their fantasies on. No. It's just that the phone rings occasionally and when I answer, there's no reply.

Katherine It's dead, do you mean?

Marion Oh, no. There's someone at the other end, all right. But the moment I speak, they hang up. It's happened several times now.

Katherine Have you reported it?

Marion (*smiling*) What's to report? It's more of an annoyance than anything.

Katherine All the same ...

Laura enters R, *followed by Michael. She carries a bright headscarf*

Laura Look what I've got. (*She displays the headscarf*)

Marion (*admiringly*) Now, isn't that pretty.

Katherine He insisted on bringing you something. I hope it's all right. It took him ages to decide on it.

Laura (*forcing a smile*) I don't know what I've done to deserve it. He only met me for a minute or two.

Marion (*knowingly*) It's the uniform that did it. You mark my words. There's many a man's head been turned by a pretty nurse.

Katherine (*amused*) I don't think you're right this time, Miss Bishop. (*To Laura*) You weren't even wearing it, were you? (*To Marion*) We were just leaving to catch our train. (*To Laura*) All the same, you did make a big impression. You got more than Mrs Meacham did, and she's known him since he was a baby.

Laura I'm flattered. (*She glances at Michael*)

Michael smiles at her

Katherine (*putting her cup down*) What do you think about these phone calls, Nurse Vinnecombe? Don't you think they need reporting?

Laura (*looking away from her*) It's difficult to say. I mean, they're not abusive in any way, apparently. If I were to speak honestly, I'd say it was children. You know what they are these days. (*She looks at Katherine as though daring her to challenge this*)

Katherine (*unconvinced*) Well ... perhaps you're right. But I can't see what they hope to gain from it. It's just a waste of their money.

Laura I shouldn't think that would worry them. Children have far too much money these days. When one considers what doting parents splash out to buy little Jimmy or Jessie a video machine or personal computer for a fourth or fifth birthday present, a few pence for the telephone is peanuts.

Katherine (*firmly*) Well if anyone starts making funny phone calls whilst *I*'m here, they'll get a very nasty surprise.

Laura (*frowning*) I'm sorry?

Katherine (*to Marion*) I've been thinking over what you asked me, and I'm willing to give it a try if you still want me.

Marion Oh, I am glad. Maybe you can help shake me out of my lethargy. (*To Laura*) Before she went away I asked her to do some typing for me. If I don't have to worry about the physical effort of writing, I might be able to make the mental effort. I can dictate on to a cassette when I feel up to it, and she can type it out for me later. With any luck I can finish *The Candle and the Moth* before I give up the ghost.

Katherine (*laughing uneasily*) Don't talk like that. You're good for another few years, yet. Time to write a dozen more.

Marion (*shaking her head*) My dear. I know I'm a romantic, but I'm also a realist. I'm seventy-one—almost seventy-two—and I've had two serious heart attacks. I could be dead by this time next month. That's why I want to complete this book. I hate leaving things half-done.

Katherine Seventy-one's no age these days, Miss Bishop.

Marion I know it isn't. But the thought of living another ten years or so as an invalid frightens the life out of me. If I can't be a healthy seventy-one, I'd rather be a dead one.

Laura Miss Bishop ...

Marion Oh, I don't relish the idea of dying. Who does? But what I'm trying to say is that I want all my loose ends tied up before I go. Make certain my affairs are in order. Knowing I'm on a knife-edge gives me the opportunity to do that, doesn't it? I've had two warnings. There may not be a third.

Katherine Well ... looking at it like that, I suppose you're right.

Marion It's no use me trying to fool myself. In a way I consider myself fortunate. Most people are totally unprepared for death. Look at that poor Nurse Ledston, for instance.

Laura's eyes open wide and she stares at Marion

Do you think she was expecting to die when she set off for work that morning?

Katherine (*frowning*) Who?

Marion The woman I was telling you about. The one they found murdered in Surrey.

Laura looks as though she's about to faint

Laura Would anyone like some more tea? (*She stuffs the headscarf in her pocket*) Katherine?
Katherine Oh, not for me, thanks. (*She looks at Marion*)
Marion (*shaking her head*) Perhaps Michael . . .

As Laura turns blindly away to exit R, *Michael, who during this interchange has wandered idly up to the window* L, *begins making excited noises*

Katherine Wasn't that the name of——

Michael lets out a yell of delight, hurries to the front door, dashes into the porch and exits L, *his voice rising*

(*Rising*) Michael.
Laura (*looking out of the window* L) It's all right. It's Dr Thorne. He's just arriving.

A car is heard to pull up, off and a moment later the car door slams

Katherine (*to Marion*) We'd better be going.
Marion No, no. Stay as long as you like. He's only come to give me another of his check-ups. It shouldn't take more than fifteen minutes. If you'll just give me a hand . . . (*She begins to rise*)
Katherine (*quickly*) Of course. (*She assists Marion to stand*)

Andrew and Michael pass the window L *then enter the porch and come into the room*

Andrew (*to Katherine, smiling*) Welcome back to civilization. Have a nice time?
Katherine Lovely, thank you.
Andrew Bet you forgot my bottle of Scotch, didn't you?
Katherine Not at all. It's only a miniature bottle, but we've got it at home for you. You can have it tomorrow.
Andrew (*to Michael*) So that's what you've been trying to tell me, is it? (*He winks at Michael*) Hello, Miss Bishop. (*To Laura*) Nurse. (*He hands her his case*) Hope you don't mind my coming along today but I have to go up to London tomorrow. It was a bit unexpected, so I thought I'd better give you a once-over before I went. How are you?
Marion Oh, bearing up, I suppose. But I'd be happier if I felt a bit more lively.
Andrew (*smiling*) Well, we'll see what we can do about that. Come on. Into your bedroom. (*He goes to the door* R *and opens it for Marion*)

Andrew and Marion exit

Katherine (*to Michael*) Well . . . we'll go and have a look round the garden, shall we? See how it's fared whilst we've been away. Might blow some of the cobwebs away, too, eh? (*She takes Michael's arm and is about to go when she halts, slightly puzzled. To Laura*) There was something I was going to ask you, but I've forgotten what it was, now. (*She gives a little laugh*) It was on the tip of my tongue a few minutes ago. (*She shakes her head*) Oh, well, I expect I'll remember. (*To Michael*) Come on.

Katherine and Michael exit. A moment later we see them pass the window R

Laura stands there biting her lip, a peculiar expression on her face

The door R *opens and Andrew appears*

Andrew Forgot my case. (*He holds his hand out for it*)
Laura Andrew. We've got to talk.
Andrew Not now. She's waiting for me.
Laura They've found Dorothy.
Andrew (*after a short silence*) Found her?
Laura I heard Miss Bishop telling Katherine about ten minutes ago. It must have been on the radio.

They look at each other in silence

Andrew (*slowly*) Is there any chance they——
Laura (*her composure cracking*) Andrew. (*She clutches hold of him*)
Andrew It's all right. It's all right. Just give me time to think. (*He holds her*)
Laura (*suddenly*) Katherine. She's remembered. I know she has. I know it. She almost came out with it. (*Desperately*) What are we going to do?
Andrew (*firmly*) Nothing. If she says anything to you, just deny it. Tell her it's a coincidence. There must be dozens of nurses called Ledston.
Laura (*dazedly*) They'll find me. I know they will. Oh, God. (*She puts her hand to her face in torment*)
Andrew Look. Ask her to come over here tonight. Tell her you've got to go out. Meet me in *The Thatched Barn* at Bempton. Nine o'clock.
Laura (*anxiously*) Can't you collect me?
Andrew We can't afford to be seen together. Not round here, anyway. Bempton's far enough away to cut down the odds.
Laura How do I get there?
Andrew Ask if you can borrow Miss Bishop's car. She can't drive it herself, so she'll probably be glad of it getting a run. Tell her you're going to meet an old friend who's staying in Longbridge. It's about the same distance but in the opposite direction.
Laura (*numbly*) I'll try.
Andrew Relax. It'll be all right. (*He gives her a quick hug and a smile*) Nine o'clock. *Thatched Barn*, Bempton.

He takes his case and exits R

Laura stands still, then slowly moves to the coffee table and starts collecting the tea things together

Katherine passes the window R *and enters from the front door. She carries a packet of cigarettes*

Katherine (*puzzled*) Nurse?
Laura (*picking up the tray, turning to her*) Yes?
Katherine You don't smoke, do you?
Laura No. Why?
Katherine I found these inside the summer-house. A packet of cigarettes.
Laura (*crossing* R) Probably been in there for years.

Katherine No. I was in there a fortnight ago. We had our lunch. They weren't there then.

Laura (*after a pause*) Perhaps they're Dr Thorne's? He was in the garden a few days ago.

Katherine Oh, I don't think so. I don't believe he smokes, either.

Laura Maybe he's just secretive about it? You know what doctors are? Smoke like chimneys themselves, but tell everyone else they shouldn't do it. I should just leave them on the table. If they are his, he'll collect them when he's finished with Miss Bishop.

Laura exits R

Katherine looks at the cigarettes for a moment, then moves to the table by the window and puts the packet down. She then moves to the fireplace and stands there looking thoughtful. The telephone rings. She moves to answer it

Laura suddenly appears R

It's all right. I'll get it. (*On the phone*) Hello? Hanbury double five four nine three. Nurse Vinnecombe speaking. . . . No. . . . Yes. Yes, of course. . . . (*She glances sharply at Katherine*) No. That'll be fine Mrs Meacham. Exactly as last week. . . . Well, perhaps an extra packet of tea then. . . . Yes. Yes. Thank you. Goodbye. (*She replaces the receiver*) Groceries. I'd forgotten to phone the order through.

Katherine (*suddenly*) Those cigarettes . . .

Laura (*frowning*) Yes?

Katherine You don't think there could be any connection between them and the telephone calls, do you?

Laura I—don't quite follow you.

Katherine (*embarrassed*) Well . . . someone watching the place, perhaps.

Laura (*forcing a smile*) I think you've been reading too many thrillers, Miss Willis. In the first place we've no proof there *have* been any phone calls. We've only Miss Bishop's word for that, and after all, we both know she's a very sick woman. It's possible she's imagined the whole thing.

Katherine I don't think that's——

Laura (*firmly*) And secondly, if someone unknown had been keeping an eye on us, why would they risk discovery by constantly phoning here? The first thing you or I would do if we intercepted the calls would be to contact the police. Isn't that so?

Katherine (*abashed*) I suppose you're right.

Laura (*smiling*) Of course I am. (*Pause*) By the way . . . there's something else I'd like to mention. I know it's none of my business, but what on earth possessed you to say you'd come out here and do typing for her?

Katherine Well . . . she was getting all upset about not being able to finish her book. And quite frankly, I can use the money.

Laura (*shaking her head*) I'm sure you meant well, but there's not a hope of her finishing it before she dies. She hasn't much time left and her mind is failing already. I'm doing my best to keep her from distressing herself, but once she realizes her concentration is going, it's the first thing that will happen. I do wish you'd change your mind.

Katherine (*helplessly*) I don't see how I can. Not now. I thought it would help. Stop her worrying about it.

Laura Instead of which, I'm afraid it's going to make things worse. It'll cause so many problems, you know.

Katherine (*softly*) I'm sorry, I didn't think.

Laura No. (*She gives her a quick smile*)

Laura exits R

Katherine stands looking forlornly after her, then turns and picks up the coats. She slips her own on as:

Doris passes the window L and appears in the porch

Doris (*brightly*) Hello, Katherine, love.

Katherine turns to face her in surprise

I hadn't realized you were home. Did you have a nice time in the wilds of Scotland? (*She enters*) I've just been over to Longbridge to pick up some odds and ends, so as I was driving past, I thought I may as well call in and see if Nurse Vinnecombe had the grocery list ready for this week. I'll give you a lift to the village if you're going that way. Save you a walk, won't it? (*She turns to the door R*) Are you there, Laura?

Katherine slowly looks at the door R

Black-out

ACT II

SCENE 1

The same. Later that evening

The room is as before, but the window curtains are closed and the main light is on. Both doors are closed. Music plays softly from the radio which is still on the coffee table. Marion sits on the settee, dozing. A thick notebook is beside her and a pencil is at her feet. After a moment, the door R opens and Laura enters. She is now dressed in a two-piece suit and blouse. She sees Marion, frowns, then crosses to her

Laura (*gently but firmly*) Miss Bishop. (*She shakes Marion's shoulder*) Miss Bishop.

Marion gives a soft, sleepy moan, and opens her eyes

It's almost eight o'clock.

Marion (*gathering her wits*) I must have dozed off. (*She glances at her watch*) Oh, my goodness.

Laura Katherine should be here at any time. Is there anything you'd like before I go?

Marion No. No. I don't think so, dear. You get off and meet your friend. I'll be all right.

Laura And you're sure you don't mind my borrowing your car?

Marion Of course not. It hasn't been out since the end of May. It's just sitting there in the garage doing nothing. Pity I didn't think of it before.

Laura Well . . . if you really don't mind . . . perhaps I could borrow it again this weekend? I could go into Longbridge and do some shopping. Stock up on groceries and things.

Marion (*puzzled*) Doesn't Doris bring us everything we need in the grocery line?

Laura Oh, yes. It's just that . . . well . . . quite frankly I think you'd be better off shopping elsewhere. I know she's very good about delivering things, but her prices are a little on the high side. You'd make considerable savings by shopping in one of the supermarkets.

Marion (*smiling*) Oh, I wouldn't dream of it, Laura. I've been a customer of hers since I moved down here. I couldn't go anywhere else. And besides, I can easily afford the extra.

Laura That's hardly the point, Miss Bishop. In my opinion you're paying out good money for something you could buy far cheaper in Longbridge. Even considering corner shop prices, you're being grossly overcharged.

Marion (*smiling*) Well, that's my problem, isn't it? Oh, don't think I'm not grateful to you. I know you're only looking after my interests, but really ... I think we'll leave things as they are. But use the car by all means. You don't have to ask.

Laura (*giving a tight smile*) If you say so, Miss Bishop. But I don't like the woman either. I don't trust her. She gossips too much.

Marion Oh, you mustn't mind her, Laura. That's just Doris. When you get to know her better, you'll find her quite fascinating. She's appeared in two of my books already, though she doesn't know it.

Laura (*forcing a smile*) I'll get my coat. (*She turns to exit* R)

Marion Oh ... would you mind bringing my pills on your way back? They're in the usual place.

Laura Of course.

Laura exits R

Marion picks up her notebook and looks around for her pencil. Seeing it on the floor, she rises and stoops to pick it up. Suddenly, a wave of dizziness sweeps over her. Eyes closed, she stands almost motionless

Laura enters with her coat on, carrying a handbag and two small bottles of tablets

(*Concerned*) Are you all right? (*She crosses quickly to her*)

Marion (*weakly*) Yes. Yes. Just a little dizzy. I must have risen too quickly. (*She opens her eyes*)

Laura Here. (*She holds on to Marion*) Sit yourself down again.

Marion allows herself to be seated. Laura drops the handbag and the bottles on to the settee

Stay still. I'll get you a glass of water.

Laura hurries out R

Marion I'll be all right. Really, I will. (*Her fingers touch the bottles. She picks them up, takes a pill from each bottle and recaps them*)

Laura hurries back with a glass of water

Laura Drink this. (*She gives the glass to Marion*)

Marion puts the pills in her mouth one at a time and washes them down with sips of water

That's better. (*She takes the glass from her*) Now I think we'd better get you to bed.

Marion (*protesting*) No. no. I'll be fine. You run along. You don't want to be late for your friend.

Laura Would you rather I stayed? I can always call and cancel.

Marion You'll do no such thing. No. You go. Katherine should be here soon. She'll see I'm all right.

Laura (*frowning*) She should have been here by now. Perhaps I should have collected her? I never gave it a thought.

Marion Oh, she's very reliable. Claims the walk keeps her healthy. You can always give her a lift home, though.

Laura Yes, there is that.

There is a knock at the door

Katherine enters breathlessly. She wears a dress beneath an autumn coat

Katherine Sorry I'm late, but there's a big party going on at The Gun and Partridge and the road's absolutely chock-a with cars. I had to keep dodging into the hedgerows to let them by. It's Gail Crosby's engagement party. (*She slips off her coat and closes the door behind her*)

Marion (*shaking her head*) Doesn't time fly? She was toddling round in her nappies when I first moved here. Such a pretty child.

Katherine (*to Laura*) All ready for the "off" then?

Laura (*doubtfully*) Well . . .

Marion (*firmly*) Of course she is. She's just worried over a dizzy spell I had a few minutes ago. But I'm all right now.

Laura If you're quite sure.

Marion I've told you. Now go. Enjoy yourself.

Laura (*relieved*) Right. I'll be on my way then. (*She indicates the glass in her hand*) I'll just take this away.

Katherine Let me. (*She takes the glass*)

Laura (*giving her a smile of thanks*) I shouldn't be too long.

Katherine There's no rush. I'll stay till you get back.

Laura picks up her bag and moves to the front door

Oh, I should take a rainhood or something. It's just started spitting and there's a wind getting up.

Laura (*hesitant*) I should be all right.

Marion You could take your headscarf. The one Michael brought back for you.

Laura Oh. Yes. Now what did I do with it? (*A short pause*) Ah. Yes. I won't be a minute.

Laura exits R

Katherine (*moving to Marion*) And what's all this about a dizzy spell?

Marion Oh, it was nothing. I stood up too quickly and it made my head spin. It happens a quite a lot these days.

Katherine Does Dr Thorne know?

Marion I suppose so.

Katherine You haven't told him?

Marion (*patiently*) My dear Katherine. I'm enough of an invalid as it is. Do you want the poor man to think he's got a hypochondriac for a patient? Anyway, I expect Laura's kept him informed. She watches me like a hawk.

Katherine It's a good job someone does. How do you feel now?

Marion As right as rain. I've even been making a few notes. (*She yawns*)

Katherine And tired yourself out by the sound of it. Don't you think it might be an idea to turn in? Have a good night's sleep? I'll help you upstairs.

Marion Oh, there's no stairs for me these days. Dr Thorne had my bed moved into the garden room. I found it there when I came out of hospital.

Katherine And that's probably all to the good. You're better off avoiding stairs if you're having dizzy spells. If you had one on the landing ...

Marion Yes, yes. I know. (*She yawns again*) Oh, dear. This is terrible.

Katherine (*kindly*) Come on. You get into your night things and I'll make you a hot drink.

Marion (*protesting*) But I want to listen to *The Merry Widow*. It's on after this and it's my favourite operetta.

Katherine I'll bring the radio through. You can listen to it in bed.

Marion (*sighing*) Oh, all right. (*She makes an effort to rise*) It's like being a slave in my own house. Do this. Do that. Bullied from pillar to post.

Katherine (*assisting her up*) Drinking chocolate or malted milk?

Marion Tea.

Marion exits R, *yawning as she goes*

Katherine (*smiling*) Tea it is.

She picks up the radio and the pill bottles and follows Marion out

A few moments later, Laura enters R, *holding a headscarf. Putting her handbag on the Welsh dresser, she puts the headscarf on, then takes a small mirror out of her bag and looks at herself. Not pleased with the result, she removes the scarf and, glancing at the door* R, *takes off her wig. She is about to replace the headscarf when:*

The front door opens and Michael enters

Laura (*spinning around to face him; startled*) You. (*Angrily*) What are you doing here?

Michael Haaaar. Haaaar. (*He makes a few steps into the room*)

Laura Hasn't anyone ever taught you to knock?

Michael (*louder*) Haaaar.

Laura touches her hair as she realizes what he is trying to say

Laura A wig. I've been wearing a wig. Haven't you ever seen one before? (*She turns quickly and crams the wig and mirror into her bag*)

Michael Haaaar.

Laura (*hissing*) Be quiet. (*She quickly goes towards him*) Keep your voice down.

Dimly realizing she is angry at him, Michael steps back, then turns and stumbles out into the night

Michael. Where are you going? Michael. Come back.

She hurries out after him

(*Off*) Michael.

A moment later, she comes back into the room, snatching her bag and headscarf and exits again, closing the door behind her

A few moments later, a car door slams, off and we hear a car moving away

The telephone begins to ring

After some moments, Katherine enters R *and answers it*

Katherine (*breathlessly*) Hello? Hanbury double five, four, nine, three. Hello? Hello? (*Her lips set in an annoyed manner and she cuts the connection. She dials the operator*) Hello? Operator? . . . This is Hanbury five, five, four, nine, three. I've just been cut off. Is there any way you can reconnect me? . . . No. It was an incoming call. . . . No, I don't know what the number was, but it was just a moment ago. . . . Can't you trace it? . . . But this isn't the first time. We keep getting them and it's most annoying. We have a sick woman here and it's very disturbing for her. . . . No, they're not obscene. They're nothing. The phone rings and when we answer it there's no-one at the other end. . . .

Marion appears R. *She is in her night-clothes*

No, it's not a fault. We can hear breathing. But there must be something you can do. It's absolutely ridiculous.

Marion Is something wrong?

Katherine (*on the phone*) All right. Yes. Yes. I'll have a word with her and we'll get back to you. Thank you. . . . Thank you. (*She hangs up*)

Marion What is it?

Katherine Another of those peculiar phone calls you've been getting, I think. I was hoping the exchange could trace it, but apparently it's not possible. If you want them to monitor all your calls for a short period, they will. But you have to make an application.

Marion (*shaking her head*) It's not worth the bother. It's all so stupid. Why do they persist? Some people have the strangest sense of humour.

Katherine And others are just sick. Still, I expect they'll tire of it eventually. Come along. I've made your drink. You don't want it to get cold, do you?

She shepherds Marion out R

For a few moments the room remains empty, then the front door opens cautiously and Raymond Shapley enters. Seeing that nobody is about, he smiles and closes the door quietly behind him. As he does so:

Katherine comes briskly in R *and lets out a startled gasp*

Raymond (*turning to face her; shaken*) Oh . . . Good-evening. (*He gives a nervous laugh*)

Katherine (*reaching blindly for the telephone*) Who are you? What are you doing here? (*She lifts the receiver*)

Raymond (*trying to recover*) Er . . . Shapley's the name. Raymond Shapley. (*He holds out his hand*) Marion Bishop's my aunt.

Katherine (*with relief*) Oh . . . I'm terribly sorry. I wasn't expecting you and I thought . . . well . . . it doesn't matter. Do excuse me. (*She puts the receiver down*)

Raymond (*relaxing*) There's nothing to excuse. I must have frightened the
daylights out of you. I hadn't realized there was anyone else here

Katherine (*smiling weakly*) Well ... it is a bit remote out here. I'd no idea
you were expected. I've been away for a while and only got back today.
Nurse Vinnecombe must have forgotten to tell me.

Raymond Vinnecombe? The ... er ... lady who left just a few minutes ago?

Katherine That's right. She's looking after your aunt.

Raymond (*thoughtfully*) Is she? Been here long, has she?

Katherine About a fortnight. She's very efficient.

Raymond Yes. I imagine she would be. (*He smiles*) But it's not her fault. She
didn't know I was coming. No-one did.

Katherine I see.

Raymond It was a spur-of-the-moment thing. I saw her pulling away from
the house. Shot off like a bat out of hell, if you'll pardon the expression.
That's why I thought Aunt Marion must be on her own.

Katherine Oh, no. She's much too ill to be left on her own. (*Quickly*) I mean
... she's all right. She's managing to get around, but she's not what she
was two weeks ago.

Raymond (*nodding*) Taken it out of her, I expect. Must have been touch and
go, eh? That was her second attack, last month, wasn't it?

Katherine Yes. If we hadn't got back from the village when we did, she
could have died right there and then. It was a terrible shock.

Raymond I can imagine. (*He turns towards the fireplace*) Er ... what do you
think her chances are? Of making a full recovery?

Katherine (*puzzled*) Recovery? Hasn't Dr Thorne told you?

Raymond I ... er ... I haven't seen him. I haven't seen anyone, actually.
I've been abroad. I read the newspaper story on her and called the
hospital. They said she'd been discharged so I thought I'd better come
down and see her for myself. She ... er ... is my only living relative.

Katherine I'll tell her you're here. I'm sure she'll be delighted. (*She turns to
go*)

Raymond (*quickly*) Oh ... I'm not too sure about that. We ... er ... we
haven't exactly hit it off in the past, you see.

Katherine (*after a pause*) Oh ...

Raymond (*smiling*) Family squabbles. The usual sort of thing. Aunt Marion
was very attached to my mother, and when Mum and Dad separated, she
took it badly. Cut herself off from Dad and myself completely and refused
to speak to us for years. Wouldn't even come to the funeral when Dad got
killed trying to save a kiddy from a blazing house.

Katherine Oh, I am sorry.

Raymond (*moving* DL) Oh, it's all in the past. I wrote to her a few times but
she never replied. Then when I read she'd had a heart attack, I thought I'd
make one more try. So here I am.

Katherine I see.

Raymond (*curiously*) What did you mean when you asked if Dr Thorne had
told me? Told me what?

Katherine (*uncomfortably*) Well ... I'm not sure it's my place. I mean ...
I'm only looking after her while Laura ... Nurse Vinnecombe is taking a

break. Perhaps you'd better have a word with him yourself. Were you hoping to stay the night?

Raymond No, no. I'm staying at an hotel in Longbridge. I wasn't too sure of my reception here. I'll be heading back to London in the morning.

Katherine How would it be if I gave him a ring? You could have a chat with him now and he could explain everything.

Raymond (*nodding*) Sure.

She goes to the phone and dials a five-figure number. She listens for a moment, then pulls a face and replaces the receiver

Katherine It's on the ansa-phone. He must have gone out.

Raymond Well ... perhaps tomorrow, then? First thing.

Katherine I'll give you his number. Oh, wait. No. I've just remembered. He won't be here tomorrow. He's going away.

Raymond Ah. (*He smiles*) Looks like you'll have to tell me, then.

Katherine (*doubtfully*) I don't know ...

Raymond I don't want to spend the next few days worrying.

Katherine He'll be back on Saturday.

Raymond I'm flying to Canada tomorrow afternoon.

Katherine Oh.

Raymond Let's sit down and you can tell me about it.

Casting a doubtful look at the door R, *she allows herself to be led to the settee. They sit*

Now what's the problem?

Katherine (*reluctantly*) I'm not much good at this sort of thing. (*She takes a deep breath*) Your aunt's a very sick woman. She ... she hasn't got long to live.

Raymond Ticker a bit worse than they first thought, eh?

Katherine No. No, it's not that. (*Very uncomfortably*) She's got cancer.

Raymond (*surprised*) Cancer?

Katherine (*softly; looking down*) It's only a matter of time.

There is a long pause

Raymond How long have they given her?

Katherine (*quietly*) Not long. A few weeks. (*Quickly*) They've done everything they could for her, but there's no chance. She's sinking fast.

Raymond rises and moves R

Raymond There ... there's no chance of her going quicker, is there? (*Hastily*) I mean ... I can't bear to think of her in all that pain.

Katherine Oh, she's not in pain. That's the one good thing about it. She doesn't even know.

Raymond So she's dying of cancer ... and has heart trouble, too? (*In mock regret*) Poor old girl. Talk about the devil and the deep blue sea.

Katherine I can't tell you how sorry I am. She's a wonderful person.

Raymond Yes, I know. (*He sighs*) Might have been better if the heart thing had taken her right away?

Katherine (*quietly*) Yes.

Raymond I ... er ... suppose she's in bed, eh?

Katherine (*nodding*) She'd just gone when you arrived. (*She rises*) Would you like to see her? She's only listening to the radio.

Raymond (*quickly*) No, no. I won't go in. I've found out what I wanted to know. (*He gives a wry smile*) I didn't realize how ill she was. Under the circumstances, seeing me here might get her all worked up again and I'd hate her to have another heart attack on my account.

Katherine I'm sure there'd be no risk of that.

Raymond All the same, I think I'll give it a miss. Another one could finish her off completely, wouldn't you say?

Katherine (*uncertainly*) Well ... it's possible, I suppose. But ...

Raymond (*shaking his head*) It's better this way. I'll call you as soon as I get back from Canada.

Katherine Oh, I won't be here ... Well ... Nurse Vinnecombe can tell you how things are. I'll explain everything to her.

The telephone rings

Excuse me. (*On the phone*) Hello? Hanbury double five, four, nine, three. Hello? Hello? (*She slams the receiver down*)

Raymond Something wrong?

Katherine Anonymous phone calls. The phone rings and there's never anyone on the other end. We'll have to report it to the police. It's getting beyond a joke. That's the second one tonight.

Raymond Why not unplug it? It's on a jack-point, isn't it?

Katherine Well ... yes. But what if there's a genuine call?

Raymond How many calls do you usually get at night?

Katherine (*after a moment's thought*) It'd make sure she wasn't disturbed, wouldn't it?

Raymond I should think so.

Katherine nods and unplugs the phone

Katherine I'd better do the extension, too. It's upstairs. I'll be back in a minute.

She exits R

Raymond (*smiling broadly*) Cancer, eh? Now there's a turn up for the books. Marion Bishop with cancer. (*He laughs quietly*) Couldn't happen to a more deserving person. (*He fumbles in his pocket for cigarettes. Not finding any, he moves over to the fireplace. He picks up an ornament, examines it thoughtfully, then slips it into his pocket. He then sits on the settee*)

Katherine enters R

Katherine There. (*She closes the door behind her*) I looked in on her but she's fast asleep. Would you care for a drink or something?

Raymond No, thanks. I ... er ... wouldn't mind a cigarette though. I seem to have run out.

Katherine I'm sorry. I don't smoke. Oh . . . wait a minute, though (*She goes to the table*) I don't know if these will be all right. (*She picks up the packet of cigarettes*) I found them in the summer-house. (*She gives them to him*)

Raymond Ah. Not . . . er . . . my usual brand, but they'll be fine. I'm not a great smoker, you understand, but I think I'm going to need one or two tonight. I can hardly take it all in. Aunt Marion with cancer. It seems incredible. I thought she'd go on forever.

Katherine gives a small smile

(*Glancing at his watch*) Well, I'd better be off. (*He rises*) Keep an eye on her for me, will you? I just wish I hadn't to leave, but I'm in the middle of a big business deal and I can't afford to let things go. Oh . . . and don't say anything to her about my visit. Let's keep it a secret between the two of us. And Nurse Vinnecombe, of course.

Katherine Well . . . if you say so.

Raymond I think it's best. (*He goes to the front door*) Cheerio. It's been nice meeting you. And thanks for the cigarettes.

He opens the door and exits

Katherine stands still for a moment, then shakes her head and goes to the settee. She sits, takes a book from the side table and begins to read

The Lights slowly fade to a Black-out to denote a passage of time; a few moments later they return to their original setting

Katherine is asleep on the settee, the open book beside her. A coffee cup and an empty plate are on the coffee table

The sound of an approaching car is heard, off. It stops and the car door slams

A few moments later, the front door opens and Laura enters. She wears her wig once more and there is no sign of the headscarf. She sees Katherine and, with a curious look on her face, moves down to gaze at her

Laura (*shaking Katherine's shoulder*) Miss Willis. Katherine.

Katherine (*waking*) Hmm? (*She struggles up to a sitting position*) Oh, I must have dropped off. (*She gives an embarrassed smile*) All that travel, I expect. (*She yawns*) Did you have a nice time?

Laura (*unfastening her coat*) Yes, thank you. I'm sorry I'm so late, but we went to the Chez Marie's in Longbridge, and you know how things are when you haven't seen someone for ages? Time passes so quickly. You just don't realize.

Katherine (*glancing at her watch*) Oh, good heavens. I didn't realize it was that time. (*She stands*) I'd better dash.

Laura I'd give you a lift, but I'm not sure I've enough petrol left to make it both ways. There's nowhere open at this time of night.

Katherine (*getting her coat*) That's all right. if the rain's stopped it'll be nice and fresh. I can be home in twenty minutes.

Laura Everything been quiet?

Katherine Not a murmur. I looked in about eleven but she was sleeping like a child. (*Suddenly*) Oh, there was one thing, though——

The sound of a car is heard, off. It pulls up and the car door slams

(*Puzzled*) Who on earth can that be at this time of night?

Laura crosses to the window L and drawing the curtains aside to peer out

Laura (*puzzled*) Looks like Mrs Meacham. Yes, it is.

There is a hammering at the front door. Laura opens it

Doris almost falls into the room. She is in a state of great agitation

Doris You haven't seen Katherine, have you? They've been looking all—— (*She catches sight of her*) Oh, Katherine. Katherine, love. (*She rushes to her and clasps hold of her tightly*)

Katherine (*taken aback*) What is it? What's wrong?

Doris I've been trying to call you for ages, but nobody answered. I thought the line was out of order.

Katherine (*realizing*) Oh, I've unplugged it. We've been getting calls . . .

Doris (*fighting back tears*) You've got to come quick, love. They've taken him to Bellingford Hospital.

Katherine (*baffled*) Who?

Doris (*beginning to cry*) Michael. He's been in a hit-and-run. They found him by the main road about an hour ago.

Katherine (*stunned*) Michael? *Michael?*

Doris (*sobbing violently*) Oh, the poor, poor boy.

Katherine (*grasping Doris and shaking her violently*) How is he? How bad is it?

Doris (*gasping and sobbing*) He's dead, love. He's dead.

Katherine (*transfixed*) No. (*Louder*) No. (*She screams*) Noooooooooooo. (*She crumples to the floor in a dead faint*)

Still sobbing, Doris sinks beside Katherine to help. Laura stands looking at them, expressionless

Black-out

SCENE 2

The same. Four days later. Morning

The room has been cleared and looks very tidy

Marion, dressed in skirt, blouse and woollen cardigan, is sitting on the settee. She is extremely pale and listless. A cassette-recorder is on the coffee table. Andrew stands looking out of the window L

Marion (*after a moment*) It's like some kind of dreadful nightmare. I keep seeing that poor boy's face. I can't get it out of my mind.

Andrew (*with a deep sigh*) No.

Marion I can't understand it. He should have been safe at home. What was he doing?

Andrew (*turning from the window*) I suppose he'd been looking for Katherine, but according to the police, he was heading *back* to the village when the car hit him.

Marion Then where had he been? He certainly didn't come here, and apart from Hanson's farm, there's nothing else on this road

Andrew Well . . . that's for the police to work out. But whoever it was that killed him, they've got a nasty dent in the front of their car. There was broken glass all over the road. It's definitely a garage job.

Marion Poor Katherine. I'll remember that scream till my dying day. How is she?

Andrew Still under sedation. Dr Ellison was looking in on her this morning, and I'll call in on my way back. It was quite a shock.

Marion I'll never forgive myself. Never. If it hadn't been for me, he'd still be alive. He'd have been at home with Katherine and everything would be fine. It's all my fault. All mine.

Andrew (*firmly*) Now don't be ridiculous. Michael's death had nothing to do with you. It was an accident. Pure and simple, and there's no reason you should feel otherwise.

Marion But if Katherine hadn't been here, he'd never have left the house.

Andrew And if God had given us wings, feathers and beaks, we'd all be birds.

Marion (*fretting*) I've got to do something. (*She sinks into thought for a moment, then nods to herself*) Yes. Yes. (*She looks up at Andrew*) I'm going to include her in my will. I'll make some changes. (*Eagerly*) I'll call Mr McSharry this morning. Right now, in fact.

Andrew You . . . er . . . you're sure you're not acting too hastily?

Marion (*shaking her head*) I've been thinking about it for the past two weeks and this dreadful business has brought it to a head. That girl's been like a daughter to me during my illness. Never once complained. And Michael was doing a wonderful job with the garden. Perhaps this way I can show my appreciation.

Andrew I'm sure you've already been more than generous.

Marion Oh, I don't think so. One can't pay for love and kindness. (*Firmly*) No. I want to do this. She looked after that boy for years. Long before their mother died. What life has that been for a young girl? I want to give her a chance to live life as it should be lived.

Andrew That's—very kind of you.

Marion You wouldn't mind if I left her half my estate, would you?

Andrew Half?

Marion I know I promised everything to you, but you're not a poor man, Andrew. You'd still come into a considerable sum . . . and there'd be the book royalties for the next fifty years or so, too. You could still set up that clinic you've set your heart on.

Andrew (*giving a light laugh*) My dear Miss Bishop. You don't have to plead with me. It's your money. Do what you like with it. As I've said before, I can't imagine why you want to leave me anything at all. I've done nothing to deserve it.

Marion You're a good man, Andrew Thorne, and in my opinion, goodness should be rewarded.

Andrew As my old grandmother used to say, "Goodness is its own reward".

Marion She was right ... but it doesn't pay the bills (*crossly*) I know how much setting up that clinic means to you, and you're going to do it. My money's no use to me when I'm gone. I want it to perform a useful service.

Andrew It'll do that, all right. But what's all this talk about dying? You're going to outlive the lot of us. We'll have to take you out on to the moor and shoot you, if we want to get rid of you.

Marion (*shaking her head*) You've all been very kind to me, but I know I'm failing. I haven't the energy to fight any more. I'm not eating and I'm sleeping more than I should have to. (*She smiles*) You can tell me the truth. I'm not frightened, you know.

Andrew What you really need is a good long holiday. And as soon as you're fit enough to travel, I'm going to insist you take one. You can spend a few weeks soaking up the sun, then come back and churn out another fifty or so of your best sellers. All right?

Marion (*smiling*) You're such a comfort, Andrew.

Andrew And you're a terrible patient. I'll give you something to help your appetite, and you can stop worrying about your sleeping pattern. Your heart needs all the help it can get at the moment, and sleep is the best way your body knows of giving it. Now where's our resident angel?

Marion Picking the last of the apples to send to the hospital and generally tidying up the garden. I don't know what we're going to do with it now. It was starting to look so nice.

Andrew Yes. (*Briskly*) Well ... you carry on with your dictating and I'll nip out and have a quick word with her. Won't be a minute.

Marion leans forward and turns the cassette-recorder on as Andrew turns towards the front door

Laura passes the window R. She is wearing her uniform and carrying a basket of apples

Ah ... no need. Here she comes.

Laura (*entering*) Oh, Good-morning, Doctor.

Andrew Good-morning, Mistress Gwynne.

Laura Apples, not oranges. (*She smiles*) I didn't hear you arrive. I was at the bottom of the garden. (*She displays the fruit*) Look at these. They're absolutely beautiful, aren't they? (*To Marion*) I'll need a ladder to get at the rest, but these should fill the last box. (*To Andrew*) We're sending them to Bellingford Hospital.

Andrew So Miss Bishop's been saying. I'm sure they'll be delighted. There's always been a good crop from Moor View. The locals call it the original garden of Eden.

Laura Yes ... and I think I discovered its serpent this morning. (*She glances down at her ankle*)

Marion You found a snake?

Laura Oh, no. Nothing as exciting as that. Just a trap for the unwary. I put my foot through a wooden cover behind the summer-house and almost fell down a hole. What is it? An old well, or something?

Marion Oh, my goodness. (*Her hand flies to her mouth*) I intended having it filled in years ago but never quite got round to it. It's at least sixty feet deep. You put your foot through it, you say?

Laura The boards are absolutely rotten.

Marion (*concerned*) Oh, Andrew. Perhaps you'd better have a look at it for me? If it's in a bad state, I'd better have something done to it before there's an accident.

Andrew Don't worry. We can have a new cover fitted without any problem.

Laura I'll go wipe these down before I pack them. Would anyone care for tea or coffee whilst I'm in there?

Marion Not for me, thank you. I don't think I could face more liquid at the moment. To tell you the truth, I'm starting to feel a bit queasy.

Andrew (*frowning*) You are? (*He moves to her and checks her pulse*) Take your tablets this morning?

Marion Of course.

Laura On the dot.

Andrew Hmm. (*To Marion*) Any tightening round the chest? Pain?

Marion No. No. Nothing like that. Just a vague feeling of sickness.

Andrew (*thoughtfully*) Probably getting yourself worked up about this hit-and-run business again. I think a little lie-down might be indicated.

Marion (*protesting*) I shall soon be spending the entire day in bed.

Andrew And you'll be none the worse for it. Give nature a chance to do her work. (*To Laura*) Nurse.

Laura (*smiling*) I'll turn the sheets back.

Laura exits R with the basket

Andrew helps Marion to her feet

Marion (*suddenly*) What about Mr McSharry? I'd like to see him as soon as possible.

Andrew You've got the rest of the day to contact him. But if you're really anxious about it, I'll drop into his office when I go back, and ask him to contact you before he goes to lunch. Will that make you happy?

Marion (*reluctantly*) I suppose so. (*With a bit of spirit*) But just you wait till I'm feeling stronger, Andrew Thorne. You won't find it so easy to order me around.

Andrew (*laughing*) Oho! The gypsy's warning.

Andrew escorts Marion out R

A few moments later, Laura enters and goes to the settee. With anxious glances at the door, she waits for Andrew to return

At last he does so, quietly closing the door behind him

Laura hurries to him and they embrace

Laura (*head on his shoulder*) Oh, Andrew. Thank God you're back. I've been worried sick.

Andrew Arrived about half an hour ago. (*He gently frees himself*) What a mess.

Laura Did you find out anything?

Andrew Not from Chris. I tried phoning several times, but no-one answered. But from what I can gather, you're quite safe. Nobody's made any connection between you and Dorothy Ledston, so if you were seen together, they're keeping very quiet about it. (*He chucks her under the chin*) Now come on. Cheer up. No news is good news.

Laura (*moving away fretfully*) Andrew. I'm worried.

Andrew Look——

Laura When I got in on Tuesday night, Katherine had the phone unplugged. She told the Meacham woman they'd been getting calls. That's why she'd done it. Chris must have phoned while we were out.

Andrew So?

Laura We'd already spoken earlier in the day. There'd be no reason to call again unless something had happened. You know the arrangement.

Andrew You mean . . .

Laura They've managed to trace me.

Andrew (*firmly*) No. It's impossible. We've covered your tracks too well.

Laura (*shaking her head*) Somebody knows I'm here.

Andrew (*grasping hold of her shoulders*) Now stop it. They couldn't do.

Laura Then what about the cigarettes in the summer-house? How did they get there? Whose were they?

Andrew Probably some old tramp's who'd been dossing down for the night.

Laura Or someone who'd been sent to keep an eye on me. (*Anxiously*) I've got to get away from here, Andrew. I've got to move.

Andrew (*sharply*) Don't be ridiculous. Where would you go? Back to London? They'd track you down inside a day. You're absolutely safe here, I promise you. By this time next month, you'll be on the other side of the world and out of their reach forever.

Laura And what about you? (*Anxiously*) You haven't changed your mind?

Andrew Of course I haven't. I'll have to stay on here for a while, though. Tidy things up et cetera. Sell my share of the practice. But I'll be joining you as soon as it's humanly possible. With the money I've got coming to me, we can both make a fresh start. A few more months and we'll be on easy street.

Laura (*relieved*) Oh, Andrew. I don't know what I'd have done without you.

Andrew You'd have coped. You're a survivor, Laura. Always have been. Now I suggest you go in and see if our patient needs anything. I'll be back later with a little something for her appetite.

Laura Do you think it's worth it?

Andrew (*shaking his head*) Hardly. A few more days and food will be the last thing on her mind. (*He smiles*) Still, we have to go through the motions. (*He moves to the front door*) See you in a few hours.

Laura (*impulsively*) Andrew . . .

Andrew Yes?

Laura Do you think I should try? To get hold of Chris? I've got to know what's happening.

Andrew (*shaking his head*) Leave it with me. I'll call as soon as I get back to the surgery. I'd rather you kept away from the phone except for local calls. Just in case. (*He opens the door*)

The sound of a car is heard, off, as it pulls up

Doris Meacham, by the sound of it. I'd better be off. See you this afternoon.

Laura (*reluctantly*) All right. But call me as soon as you hear something.

Andrew I will. Promise.

Doris passes the window L, *and enters the porch. She carries a box of groceries, but is far from her usual smiling self*

Doris (*wanly*) Morning, Doctor.

Andrew Morning, Doris. (*He stands aside to let her pass*) I'll drop that medicine in later, then, Nurse. Good-morning.

Andrew exits, closing the door behind him. After a few moments, we see him pass the window L

A car door slams, off and the car moves away

Doris (*subdued*) I'm sorry I'm late. I called in to see how Katherine was.

Laura And . . . how is she?

Doris Still in a state of shock. Dr Ellison was in to see her earlier, but I'm not sure it did her much good. Not surprising really. It's not every day you have one of your family murdered, is it?

Laura (*suddenly still*) Murdered?

Doris Hadn't you heard? Whoever it was ran him down, didn't manage to kill him outright. They finished him off by drowning him in the ditch.

Laura (*impatiently*) Really, Mrs Meacham . . . Wherever did you hear a story like that?

Doris (*flatly*) The police found the marks and things where the car had stopped. The driver went back to check on him, from the look of things, because the grass was all trampled down where he'd been dragged over it and rolled into the water.

Laura (*turning away*) That's horrible. I can't believe it.

Doris All I hope is that the poor lad knew nothing about it. I couldn't bear to think he'd . . . If it hadn't been for Hanson's old collie, he could have been in there for days. It was Mrs Hanson called the police. They took him to Bellingford but nobody knew where Katherine was. It was me who suddenly thought she might be here. Poor girl. It'll be a long time before she gets over this. Michael was all she had.

Laura Yes.

Doris I just can't take it in. None of us can. Who'd want to murder a young lad like him? He wouldn't hurt a fly.

Laura No.

Doris I've always been against capital punishment, but after this, I could cheerfully put the rope around his neck myself. Funny how you can change your opinions when things strike close to home, isn't it? I keep thinking how I'd feel if it were my Brian. (*She gives a deep sigh*) Oh, well. I'd best be getting back. I'll see you next week. (*She turns to go*)

Laura (*suddenly*) Oh, Mrs Meacham.

Doris stops and looks at her

I ... er ... I don't know that we'll be requiring anything else for a while. Miss Bishop's not eating too well, and there seems to be plenty in the cupboards. It's silly just to stockpile things. I'll let you know if there's anything we are short of.

Doris (*frowning*) You mean ... you won't be wanting an order?

Laura (*smiling*) That's right.

Doris Oh. (*She looks uncertainly at Laura*) Well ... you know best, of course. But you've got the number, haven't you. It won't take me a minute to bring things up. It's no trouble.

Laura I'm sure it isn't. But I wouldn't dream of bothering you. I'll come down to the village. The walk will do me good and it'd give me the chance to look round.

Doris Depends on what you find yourself needing. If it's anything heavy, you'd be better off asking if you can borrow the car again.

Laura (*startled*) Car?

Doris Miss Bishop's old Rover. It was you over in Bempton, Tuesday night, wasn't it?

Laura Bempton?

Doris At *The Thatched Barn*? (*She smiles wryly*) Oh, you can't keep a secret round these parts for long. George Lake spotted the car in the forecourt. About half-past nine. He used to do part-time chauffering for her before he had his stroke. Recognized it at once.

Laura (*coldly*) Really? (*She forces a smile*) Well I'm afraid he must have been mistaken. I did borrow the car Tuesday night, but I was over in Longbridge. With a friend. At Chez Marie's.

Doris Oh. (*Off balance*) It's not like him to make a mistake.

Laura To err is human, as they say.

Doris I suppose so. But he was quite definite about it.

Laura (*sharply*) I could give you the name of my friend.

Doris (*quickly*) Oh, no. No. There's no need for anything like that. I'm not doubting your word. (*She smiles*) You know what men are like about cars, don't you? Think they know it all. I mean, you could hardly be in two places at once could you?

Laura No.

Doris Right. Well. I'll be off then. We'll see you when we see you.

Laura stares at her without replying

Doris gives Laura an uncertain smile and exits leaving the front door open. A moment later, she passes the window L

Laura moves to the table and stands

A car door slams, off and the car moves away

Laura picks up the box of groceries and exits into the kitchen

A moment later, Raymond passes the window R *to appear in the porch soon after. He enters the room and, with a smile on his face, he waits for Laura to return*

Laura enters. On seeing Raymond she halts in her tracks

Raymond (*affably*) Good-morning.

Laura (*sharply*) Who are you?

Raymond (*smiling*) Well, now. That's really a question *I* should be asking, isn't it?

Laura (*at a loss*) I beg your pardon?

Raymond (*smiling*) According to local information, you're Laura Vinne-combe. A private nurse from London.

Laura (*defensively*) That's right. I am. What about it?

Raymond (*moving* L; *easily*) Silly, isn't it? I had the distinct impression you were somebody totally different. In fact ... had anyone asked me, I'd have sworn you were Laura *Sanderson*. (*He smiles*)

Laura (*shaken*) Then it's a good job no-one did ask, isn't it, Mr——?

Raymond Shapley. Raymond Shapley.

Laura For your information, Mr Shapley, I've never heard of Laura Sanderson, so if you wouldn't mind lea——

Raymond Then I don't expect you've heard of Dorothy Ledston, either have you?

Laura (*fighting panic*) No. I don't believe I have. Who is she?

Raymond She's the lady whose uniform you happen to be wearing. I took the liberty of examining your room on Tuesday night—just after you went out. (*He smiles charmingly*)

Laura (*amazed*) You did *what*?

Raymond (*sitting on the settee arm*) I climbed in through the bedroom window. Oh, I didn't disturb anything. I've had quite a lot of practice in housebreaking. I just checked up on a few things. Tut, tut, tut. Very careless of you to leave her name-tag still inside. With your connections, I'd have given you more credit.

Laura (*coldly*) Mr Shapely. I haven't the faintest idea of what you're talking about, but if my uniform does happen to have someone else's name-tag sewn inside, it's hardly surprising. If you knew anything about the nursing profession, you'd know we're notoriously underpaid for the work we do. Several of us do own second-hand uniforms.

Raymond (*nodding*) Ah, I see. And it's just coincidence that you happen to be wearing one belonging to a nurse who was found strangled in Surrey a few days ago?

Laura Of course it is. What else could it be?

Raymond Hmm. Then I assume it's just another coincidence that the local police are looking for the hit-and-run driver who killed the village idiot four nights ago, and Marion Bishop's car—which is tucked away inside her garage—has a somewhat crumpled wing and a broken headlight?

Laura (*startled*) How——

Raymond I took the liberty of forcing the garage door. (*He smiles*)

Laura (*icily*) I don't know who or what you're supposed to be, Mr Shapley, but before I throw you out, there's something you should know. I damaged the door on Tuesday evening by trying to manoeuvre it out of a parking space on a crowded restaurant forecourt. I somehow managed to hit a concrete gatepost, and if needs be, can produce a witness to verify the fact. Now get out, and don't ever let me see you near this place again. (*She marches to the door and stands there waiting*)

Raymond (*rising*) As you wish. Good-morning, Mrs Sanderson.

Laura (*coldly*) Goodbye, Mr Shapley. And the name is Vinnecombe.

Raymond Ah, yes. So you told me. (*He smiles*) In that case, I ... er ... don't suppose you'll mind me contacting "certain parties" and showing them the photographs I took of you when I thought you were Mrs Sanderson? The resemblance is quite amazing—apart from the hair colour, of course. I'm sure they'll be as surprised as I am to find it's a case of mistaken identity.

Laura Photographs?

Raymond (*taking a few snapshots from his pocket*) Not exactly Lord Snowdon standards, but clear enough under the circumstances. (*He hands them to her*) Taken from inside the summer-house.

Laura (*looking at them in dismay*) It was you.

Raymond (*frowning*) You saw me?

Laura You left your cigarettes behind.

Raymond Oh, yes. Careless of me, wasn't it? (*He indicates the snaps*) Keep them if you like. I still have the negatives.

Laura (*after a moment*) How did you find me?

Raymond Find you? (*He pretends to understand*) Ah. Then you *are* Laura Sanderson?

Laura (*tightly*) Yes, damn you. Now answer me.

Raymond Believe it or not—as Mr Ripley once said—it was quite by accident. I came down here to try and get money from my aunt. She's Marion Bishop, by the way.

Laura You're lying. She has no relatives. Dr Thorne's asked her.

Raymond (*shaking his head*) You don't want to believe everything she tells you, Mrs Sanderson. Her late sister was my mother, but she refuses to acknowledge me because of my wild and wicked ways. She doesn't hold with crime and violence. Quite funny, really, when you consider she's got you looking after her. I'd love to see her face if ever she found out the truth. (*Quickly*) But you needn't worry. I've no intention of telling her.

Laura That's very considerate of you.

Raymond Oh, I'm a considerate person. Ask anyone—except Aunt Marion, of course. But as I was saying, I came down here to get my hands on some badly needed cash, and almost the first person I laid eyes on was you. It was a good disguise. I'll give you that. The wig and uniform had me fooled for quite a while. But there was something about the face. You're very attractive, Mrs Sanderson. No wonder Dave fell for you.

Laura You work for Dave?

Raymond (*shaking his head*) No, but I know of him. Who doesn't? Now the Wilmot boys are inside, he's the kingpin, isn't he. The old man's retired and young Reg is nothing more than a psychopathic "pusher" . . . though don't tell him I said so. I'd hate to meet him in a dark alley some night or share a cell with a couple of his boys.

Laura You've been in prison, then?

Raymond Once or twice. That's where I first saw your picture. Front page of the *Mirror*. You were coming out of the registry office on your wedding-day. (*He smiles*) You ended up on half the walls in Wandsworth. It's one of the reasons I remember you so well. My cell-mate had you taped to the wall by his bed. You were the last thing I saw at night before I went to sleep.

Laura (*drily*) I'm flattered.

Raymond I watched you for two or three days. Trying to puzzle out where I'd seen you before. Even introduced myself to the dummy's sister, but it didn't get me anywhere—apart from finding out an interesting thing or two about Aunt Marion's health. Finally I took a chance and slipped back inside here to check your things. You almost fooled me again. Finding the Ledston woman's name inside that uniform was a bit of a shock. I'd never met anyone of that name in my life. And then I remembered. The nurse found strangled in Surrey.

Laura And you put two and two together?

Raymond Wouldn't you have done? I hung around that night, waiting for you to get back. As soon as I saw you fitting that wig before you came in here, all the pieces fell into place. You were Dave Sanderson's wife. The one everybody was looking for. And I'd found you.

Laura (*turning away; very controlled*) And what do you intend doing with your knowledge, Mr Shapley?

Raymond That all depends on you.

Laura (*icily*) If that's supposed to mean what I think it means . . .

Raymond (*shaking his head*) It doesn't. All I'm after is a little assistance. After all—I wouldn't like to get on the wrong side of Dave and Co, now would I? No-one knows better than you what he's capable of when something upsets him. (*He smiles*)

Laura (*after a moment*) What kind of assistance?

Raymond Assistance in getting my hands on what's rightfully mine. Marion Bishop has six hundred thousand pounds of my money. It's tied up in a trust fund, and I'm not going to see a penny of it until she dies. She's made that perfectly clear, the old bitch.

Laura I see.

Raymond There could be more . . . I haven't been able to get hold of her will to check . . . but the deal's this. If you're willing to help me, then no-one on God's earth will find out from me where you're hiding. (*He pauses*) There'll also be a nice spot of cash for you as a kind of bonus.

Laura And what do you want me to do?

Raymond I hear she's got cancer. Hasn't long to live?

Laura That's true.

Raymond She must be taking something for it. Some kind of drug?

Laura nods

Supposing she took an overdose? Quite by accident. What would happen? Would she die?

Laura It's—possible.

Raymond (*eyes narrowing*) Only *possible*? Come on. You can do better than that, can't you?

Laura Very well, then. She'd die.

Raymond (*relaxing*) Yes. That's what I thought. And nobody would be suspicious?

Laura Why should they be? They're expecting it at any time.

Raymond Then what do you say?

Laura (*after a moment*) Let me get this straight. In return for your silence—and a "nice spot of cash"—you want me to kill your aunt? A woman who's going to be dead within the next few weeks anyway. What's the hurry?

Raymond I can't afford to wait that long. I need money fast. I'm in it up to here. (*He indicates his neck*) Will you do it, or won't you?

Laura I . . . don't know. I'll have to think about it.

Raymond (*sneering*) Don't tell me you've got cold feet. You've killed two people already. A sick old woman isn't going to be any problem.

Laura No. But a rather aggrieved doctor might well be.

Raymond Doctor? You mean the one from the village? What's *he* got to do with it?

Laura (*laughing harshly*) My dear Mr Shapley. He's got everything to do with it. You don't think I'm down here by chance, do you? Andrew and I were lovers for years before I met Dave Sanderson, but we lost track of each other when he had to leave London. After I walked out on Dave, I moved in with Dorothy Ledston for a few days. We'd trained at the Westminster Hospital together. She told me she was coming down here to help Andrew out . . . looking after your aunt. I asked her to change places with me. To let me come in her place. But she refused. I think she fancied her chances with Andrew and didn't want me to start renewing "auld acquaintance" with him.

Raymond So you killed her. For that?

Laura (*smiling*) Oh, no. There was much more to it than that. You see, I contacted Andrew and found out his plans. I told you we were very close. (*Sweetly*) Did you know that every penny of your aunt's will come to him when she dies?

Raymond (*startled*) What?

Laura According to her, she had no living relatives, so who better to leave it to than her faithful friend the doctor, who dreamed of setting up his own clinic for medical research. (*She laughs*) The poor old fool. As if Andrew would waste his money on something like that. Oh, no. He's got far better plans in mind. All I had to do was to make sure she had a slight overdose every time she took her medication—just enough to keep her drowsy—and to make sure she never had the opportunity to change her will again. Of course, I didn't want Dave or anyone else to know where I was. Hence the disguise and change of name ... but I never expected the "dummy", as you call him, to see me without my wig. I'd no way of knowing if he could pass the information to that goody-goody sister of his, so I had to get rid of him too. (*Slowly*) And now *you*'ve turned up.

Raymond (*suddenly wary*) You would be thinking of ...

Laura (*smiling coldly*) No, Mr Shapley. Not while you've still got those negatives tucked safely away. But I'll have to speak to Andrew. If it's only the six hundred thousand pounds you want, you're welcome to it. But if it's the rest of the money ...

Raymond (*relaxing*) You don't have to worry. I'll settle for what's mine.

Laura How can I contact you? If Andrew agrees?

Raymond I'm staying at the Green Dragon in Longbridge. Under the name of Dickenson. If I'm out, you can leave a message.

Laura Very well. I'll call you as soon as I've spoken to him.

Raymond (*grinning*) I'll look forward to hearing from you.

He opens the front door and exits

Laura closes the door, then turns to face front, her face a mask. After a moment, she goes to the telephone, lifts the receiver and dials a five-digit number

Laura (*on the phone*) Hello? Surgery? ... This is Nurse Vinnecombe. Moor View. Is Dr Thorne there by any chance? ... Would you? ... Oh, thank you. (*Pause*) Andrew? ... It's Laura. I've got to see you. As soon as possible. ... Yes, I know you are, but it won't wait. I've just had a visitor. Miss Bishop's mysterious nephew. ... Yes. That's right. Raymond Shapley. He wants us to murder his aunt.

Black-out

SCENE 3

The same. The following day. Evening

The room is as before, but the cassette-recorder has been removed from the coffee table. The curtains are drawn and the main light is on

Laura sits on the settee gazing into the fire. Andrew enters and she turns her head to look at him

Laura Is everything ready?

Andrew (*nodding*) Where is she?

Laura Sleeping.

Andrew Good. That'll make it a lot easier. The less she knows about it, the better.

Laura What about afterwards? When it's all over?

Andrew We go on as planned. (*He moves behind her and rests his hands on her shoulders*) Don't worry. Nothing will go wrong.

Laura (*touching his hand*) No.

Andrew Do you want to run over it again? Just to be sure?

Laura (*shaking her head*) No. I'll be all right once we've started. It's just the waiting.

Andrew (*briskly*) How about a drink of something?

Laura I wouldn't say no to a stiff brandy.

Andrew No sooner said ... (*He goes to the dresser and pours out a couple of drinks*)

There is a knock at the front door

Putting down the decanter, Andrew glances at his watch, frowns and shakes his head at Laura

He slips quietly out of the door R

Laura rises and goes to open the door

Katherine is standing in the porch. She is deathly pale and is obviously fighting to control herself. She wears a heavy coat with deep pockets

Laura (*surprised*) Katherine.

Katherine May I come in?

Laura steps aside to allow her to enter. As she closes the door again, Katherine's eyes never leave her

Laura (*uncertainly*) How are you?

Katherine (*flatly*) As well as can be expected.

Laura (*a little at a loss*) Can I get you something? A drink, perhaps? You look as though you could use one.

Katherine No, thank you. (*She continues to gaze fixedly at Laura*)

Laura (*uneasily*) Is something wrong?

Katherine I wanted to look at your face, that's all.

Laura (*puzzled*) My *face*? Why?

Katherine Isn't it obvious? To see what the face of a murderer looked like.

Laura Murderer? (*She laughs nervously*) Whatever are you talking about?

Katherine They brought Michael's things back yesterday. I couldn't bring myself to touch them until this afternoon. I found *this* in his pocket. (*She produces the headscarf he gave to Laura*) Do you recognize it?

Laura Katherine ... (*She reaches out to touch her*)

Katherine (*fiercely*) Don't touch me.

Laura draws back her hand

(*Quietly*) Why? Why did you do it?

Laura You're making a mistake. I didn't harm——

Katherine (*sharply*) I asked you a question? Why did you kill Michael?

Laura (*helplessly*) I didn't.

Katherine (*screaming*) Liar. (*Softly*) I've just been and looked at the car. (*Almost in a whisper*) Why did you kill my brother?

Laura Katherine.

Katherine (*loudly*) Why?

Laura (*firmly*) Keep your voice down. You'll waken Miss Bishop.

Katherine (*fiercely*) I don't care who I wake. You murdered my brother and I want to know why. (*She produces a large kitchen knife from her pocket*) Why? (*She moves towards Laura holding it firmly*)

Laura lets out a gasp and backs away

Andrew enters R, *his face grim*

Andrew Katherine.

Katherine looks at him in surprise

Put the knife down. Please. You're wrong. Laura didn't kill Michael. She couldn't have done. She couldn't kill anyone.

Katherine (*unyielding*) Couldn't she?

Andrew (*moving cautiously towards her*) Of course she couldn't. Give me the knife. (*He holds out his hand for it*)

Katherine And I suppose she couldn't lie, either?

Andrew (*throwing a glance at Laura*) Lie? About what?

Katherine When she got back that night, she told me she'd been to Chez Marie's in Longbridge. After I found this (*she shakes the headscarf*) I phoned them and asked. They said they'd never heard of her and couldn't even recognize the description I gave.

Laura Katherine ... Miss Willis ...

Katherine (*frighteningly quiet*) That's when it all fell into place for me. The cigarettes in the summer-house. The mysterious phone calls. That poor nurse found strangled. Everything.

Andrew You're not making sense, Katherine.

Katherine Aren't I, Doctor? Then tell me this. Did you or did you not engage a nurse by the name of Dorothy Ledston to look after Miss Bishop whilst I took Michael to Scotland?

Andrew (*after a slight pause*) Yes. That's perfectly correct. But as I told you ... she went off on another job and Nurse Vinnecombe took her place.

Katherine Did *she* tell you that? (*She indicates Laura with the knife tip*) About the other job?

Andrew (*mildly*) No. As a matter of fact, I spoke to Nurse Ledston myself. She was an old friend of mine. We'd worked together several times in the past.

Katherine And she told you she wouldn't be coming here after all?

Andrew Yes.

Katherine Then why did someone strangle her?

Laura Andrew ...

Andrew It's all right. I'll handle this. (*To Katherine*) I'm afraid I can't tell you that, Katherine. It's something we may never find out. But it's nothing to do with Laura. She was already down here when Dorothy was killed. It happened the day after you left for Scotland. Remember?

Katherine (*coldly*) And what about the phone calls? Those mysterious "no-one-at-the-other-end" ones Miss Bishop keeps getting?

Andrew What about them?

Katherine Did you know that she (*she indicates Laura again*) knew the person responsible? Oh, yes. It was rather embarrassing for her to have to answer one of them whilst I was in the room. (*To Laura*) You told me It was Doris Meacham asking for the primary cider, didn't you? But you never expected her to turn up here not two minutes after you'd put the phone down, did you? That was another lie, wasn't it?

Andrew Katherine . . .

Katherine (*softly*) I couldn't understand it. It didn't make sense. There was no need to lie to me. I wasn't interested in her private life. I had a life of my own. Had. She took it away from me. She took it from Michael, too. (*To Laura*) It was your lover, wasn't it? The man you used to meet in the summer-house. He used to call you here to arrange things.

Laura No.

Katherine I suppose he's married? Someone from the village?

Andrew You're wrong.

Katherine (*ignoring him*) Someone you were afraid to be seen with. And Michael saw you, didn't he? (*Her voice begins to rise*) He must have followed me out here that night. He saw you together and you chased him in Miss Bishop's car. You ran him down like a dog then threw him into a ditch to die, didn't you? (*She begins to shake with sobs*)

Laura No. No.

Katherine Then how did he get this headscarf?

The door R opens and Marion appears. She looks dreadful. Her face is deathly white and her lips blue. She is in her night-clothes and moves with difficulty

Marion (*weakly*) Because *I* gave it to him, dear.

All look at her in surprise

Andrew Miss Bishop. (*He looks quickly at Laura*) You should be in bed.

Marion I'm all right, Andrew. If you'll just help me to the settee.

Andrew (*taking hold of her*) You're freezing. Is your window open?

Marion (*shaking her head*) No. No, it's closed.

Andrew (*seating her*) I'll get you a blanket.

Marion There's no need. I'm not cold. Not cold at all.

Andrew (*to Laura*) Get her a cup of tea. Quickly. Plenty of sugar.

Marion I don't want any. I couldn't drink it. (*Gently*) Katherine. Come here, my dear. Sit beside me. (*She weakly pats the seat beside her*) It's all right. You've nothing to be afraid of.

Andrew and Laura exchange glances. Katherine moves to the settee and sits

I think you owe Laura an apology, my dear. She had nothing to do with Michael's death and I think I can prove it to you.

Andrew and Laura exchange glances

She'd left the house long before it happened. Don't you remember? We heard the car leave. You were helping me into my night-clothes.

Katherine (*dully*) What does that prove?

Marion (*gently taking the knife from her*) Nothing in itself, my dear . . . but I saw Michael more than two hours later.

Andrew and Laura exchange startled glances. Katherine stares at Marion in disbelief

I woke up, you see. The room was so hot. I opened the window but it didn't seem to make things any better, so I came in here to see if you'd like a drink of tea, or something. (*She smiles gently*) You were fast asleep. Worn out from your travelling, I expect. So I left you. I thought I was going to suffocate. I had to get air. I went out into the porch and just stood there, looking out over the moor and watching the stars. It was then that I saw him. Michael. Standing there by the side of the road and looking towards Bempton. I wondered what he was doing. He should have been in bed. I went to speak to him. To find out.

Andrew But——

Marion throws him a quietening look

Katherine (*to Marion*) And . . . did you?

Marion (*almost in a world of her own*) He was upset. I could see that. He kept pulling at his hair and making sounds. I couldn't understand. And then I saw it. Caught on the hedge. That headscarf you're holding.

Laura I must have dropped it when I went for the car.

Marion (*ignoring her*) I recovered it and gave it to him. He put it in his pocket, and ran off down the road towards the village. It was like a dream. It all seemed so unreal. (*More firmly*) You were still sleeping when I came back so I made myself a drink and went to bed again. I didn't know any more till your screams woke me. That was just before midnight. Almost two hours later. So you see . . . she couldn't have hurt Michael. It's an impossibility.

Katherine closes her eyes in relief and her body begins to shake with sobs again

(*Comforting her*) There, there.

Andrew Let me give you something. I've got my bag here.

Katherine (*sobbing*) No, no. I'll be all right. I'll be fine.

Laura I'll get you a brandy. (*She moves to the dresser and gets a glass of brandy. She carries it back to Katherine*) Drink this. (*She hands it to her*)

Katherine (*struggling to control herself*) I'm sorry, Laura. I don't know what I was thinking of. It just seemed that everything that's happened here, has happened since *you* arrived. And with the car being damaged . . .

Marion (*gently*) Just an unfortunate coincidence. Laura's already explained to me how that happened.

Katherine (*ashamed*) What a fool I've made of myself.

Andrew Of course you haven't. From your point of view I expect it all seemed pretty clear-cut. You'll feel better now you've got it off your chest.

Marion And you can rest assured that the person who killed Michael won't get away with it. I can promise you that. The police will soon know the truth.

Andrew glances at his watch and throws an anxious look at Laura

Katherine (*embarrassed*) Yes. I suppose they will. (*She sniffles*) I'd better be going. (*She wipes her eyes*) I'd like a little time to work out what I'm going to do now.

Laura Do?

Katherine (*rising*) Obviously I can't come back here. Not after this.

Marion Don't be ridiculous. Of course you can. I'm sure Laura won't give another thought to what's been said. (*To Laura*) Will you dear?

Laura (*smiling*) Of course not. I'm just pleased we managed to clear everything up. We'll expect you tomorrow as usual.

Katherine (*smiling wanly*) I'll—think about it.

Andrew I'll run you back to the village.

Katherine There's no need. Really.

Andrew A second-class ride is better than a first-class walk. It won't take me a couple of minutes. (*To Marion*) And you'd better go back to bed, Madam Romance. You've had a lot of excitement tonight. We don't want you having another heart attack before morning, do we?

Marion (*smiling*) I don't think there's much danger of that happening.

Laura Better safe than sorry. Don't worry, Doctor. I'll see she's tucked up by the time you get back.

Marion Back?

Andrew I ... er ... I've something I want to discuss with Nurse Vinnecombe.

Marion Oh.

Andrew (*to Katherine*) Come on, Katherine. Your chariot awaits.

Katherine (*awkwardly*) Good-night.

Andrew opens the front door

Marion (*suddenly*) Oh ... before you go, my dear. I wonder if you'd do me a favour? There's a small package at the side of my bed. Is it possible you could deliver it for me in the morning? Before you come over. It'll save me having to put a stamp on it.

Laura I'll get it for you, shall I?

Marion No, no. Katherine can get it. You can make me that cup of tea. I think I'm ready for it now.

Laura Of course. (*She smiles*)

Katherine and Laura exit R

Andrew (*to Marion*) I'd like a word with you when I get back.

Marion Yes. I thought you might.

Andrew I'll start the car up.

Andrew exits closing the door behind him

Marion sits still, staring at the knife in her hand

Katherine enters R with a small manila package

Katherine (*showing the package*) It this it?

Marion (*smiling*) That's the one.

Katherine Where would you like it delivered?
Marion Oh, to my solicitor. Mr McSharry. And wait for his reply, will you, dear?
Katherine Of course. (*She wipes her eyes*)
Marion Doctor's waiting for you outside.
Katherine Thank you. (*She kisses Marion lightly on the cheek*)

Marion hands her the knife

(*Thrusting it quickly into her pocket*) Good-night, Miss Bishop.

Almost running, Katherine exits closing the front door behind her

Marion (*softly*) Goodbye, dear.

After a moment, the car door slams, off and the car moves away

Laura enters R

Laura (*smiling*) You'd already set the tray.
Marion Yes. I made sure everything was ready.
Laura It won't take a minute for the kettle. (*She pauses*) I ... er ... I'm sorry all this had to happen.
Marion Yes.
Laura It must have been terrible for her.
Marion Yes.

There is an uncomfortable pause

Laura (*brightly*) Well ... why don't you go back to bed and I'll bring your tea through?
Marion (*thoughtfully*) No. I don't think so. I'll just stay quietly here for the moment.
Laura I did promise Doctor.
Marion Yes. I know. (*She makes no attempt to move*)
Laura Is something wrong?
Marion (*coming out of her thoughts*) Hmm? Oh, no. No. I'm just thinking.
Laura (*after a pause*) I'll check that kettle. (*She goes to the door R, stops and looks back*)

Marion has drifted away into her private world again

Laura frowns and exits

There is a short pause

Marion (*dreamily*) "Strange, is it not? that of the myriads who
Before us pass'd the door of Darkness through,
Not one returns to tell us of the Road
Which to discover we must travel too."

Laura returns with the tray of tea things, just in time to hear the last few words

Laura (*crossing to the coffee table*) Sorry?

Marion (*looking at her*) A quotation. Omar Khayyám.

Laura Oh. (*She pours out two cups of tea and hands one to Marion*) There we are. And as soon as you've finished, it's straight to bed. You need all the rest you can get

Marion smiles at her and takes a sip. She pulls a face

Is something wrong?

Marion I think the milk must be turning. It tastes peculiar.

Laura (*taking a sip of her own*) Seems all right to me.

Marion (*shaking her head*) I suppose it's all right then. It must be me. Everything tastes off these days.

Laura Perhaps your stomach's a little upset?

Marion I shouldn't be surprised. (*She sips at her tea again*)

Laura (*moving* R) I ... er ... I'd like to thank you for what you said earlier. To Katherine. If it hadn't been for you, she'd still be convinced I killed her brother.

Marion Yes. I suppose she would.

Laura (*relaxing slightly*) I couldn't believe it when she accused me. I didn't know what to say. Thank goodness you saw him after I'd left. (*She takes another drink*)

Marion Hmm? Oh ... but I didn't. (*She smiles*) I lied to her.

Laura (*taken aback*) Lied?

Marion (*sipping at her tea*) Yes. I didn't see Michael that night. I made the whole thing up. Except for the part about finding her asleep. That was true, of course. Poor girl. She looked absolutely exhausted.

Laura Then ... ?

Marion Why did I do it? (*She smiles*) I'm very fond of Katherine. She's the kind of girl I'd have wished for had I been married and had a child of my own. I didn't want her to do anything foolish—like trying to take the law into her own hands.

Laura You mean ... she might actually have attacked me with that knife?

Marion (*nodding*) There was that possibility. Yes. And I didn't want her to suffer any more than she already had done.

Laura No. No. I can understand that. (*She sips at her tea*)

Marion Besides, I felt it was my responsibility. If it hadn't been for me, three people wouldn't have lost their lives.

Laura (*staring at Marion*) Three people? I—don't understand.

Marion (*gently*) Don't you, my dear? There's really no need to keep up the pretence any longer. I know everything, you see. Why you killed that poor Nurse Ledston and ran down Michael Willis ... and what you had in mind for me.

Laura (*looking at her in shock*) I ... don't know what you mean. (*She puts her cup on the dresser*)

Marion (*calmly*) Oh? I thought perhaps you might. (*Curiously*) How were you going to do it? Murder me, I mean? Was it with an overdose?

Laura Miss Bishop——

Marion (*mildly*) It's quite all right, Laura. You can tell me. It really doesn't matter now. I'm only asking out of curiosity.

Laura (*laughing nervously*) No-one was going to murder you. With an overdose or anything else for that matter.

Marion (*smiling*) I've already told you. I *know*, Mrs Sanderson

Laura stares at her in fascinated horror

I was about to do some dictation on my book yesterday morning. The recorder was on the table here in front of me. Your entrance with the apples distracted me and I inadvertently left it running. Every word spoken in this room was recorded until the tape ran out. I discovered what had happened in the afternoon and heard your entire conversation with Dr Thorne, with Doris Meacham, and with my nephew, Raymond Shapley. Need I say more? (*She sips her tea*)

Laura (*shaking her head*) It wasn't the way it sounded. You don't understand.

Marion (*interested*) Don't I? Then why did Raymond turn up here this evening? To discuss the weather, perhaps?

Laura You ... you've seen him?

Marion (*putting her cup down*) Oh, yes. About half an hour ago.

Laura But he wasn't supposed to be here till eleven thirty.

Marion (*nodding*) I know. I heard you call him. After your telephone conversation with Dr Thorne. He was to meet you by the summer-house, I believe?

Laura Yes. But——

Marion (*holding up her hand to silence her*) This afternoon—whilst you were in the garden—I telephoned his hotel and left a message in your name. I asked him to arrive an hour earlier than agreed. (*Quietly*) I waited for him inside the summer-house. (*She smiles*) You can imagine his surprise when I stepped out of the darkness in front of him.

Laura What did he tell you?

Marion He didn't tell me anything. There wasn't really time, you see. I'd positioned myself quite carefully. When he stepped back in surprise, he went straight through the rotten boards covering the old well. It seemed a very long time before I heard the splash. (*She shakes her head*) Poor Raymond. I don't believe he ever learned to swim.

Laura (*aghast*) You mean ... he's *dead?*

Marion (*calmly*) Oh, I should think so. By this time, anyway. (*She picks up her cup again*) I came back inside just in time to hear Katherine arrive.

Laura That's why you were so cold. You'd been outside.

Marion (*voice hardening*) The cold came from *inside*, Laura. It was the cold that came when I realized what a fool I'd been. How I'd been too blind to see what was happening under my very nose.

Laura You're wrong, Miss Bishop. You're wrong. You don't know how much you're wrong.

Marion Then why don't you tell me?

Laura My being here has nothing to do with you. It's to do with *me*. (*She suddenly gags and quickly puts her hand to her mouth*) Excuse me. (*She*

pauses) I was a nurse for eight years. Probationer to ward sister. I gave it all up when I married, you see. He wanted me at home.

Marion (*nodding*) Of course.

Laura His name was Dave Sanderson. He swept me off my feet. Gave me everything towels, furs, my own car. It was another way of life to me. Another world. We were married six weeks after we met.

Marion Like Cinderella? From rags to riches.

Laura Exactly. (*She gags again*)

Marion (*mildly*) Is something wrong?

Laura (*swallowing hard*) A touch of nausea, that's all. I'm sorry. (*She takes a deep breath*) It wasn't until the following morning . . . when I read the papers . . . that I found out who Dave Sanderson really was. He was one of Gangland's most vicious criminals with fingers in armed robbery, prostitution, drug smuggling and God knows what else. I couldn't believe it. I wouldn't believe it. I was sure it was all some dreadful mistake. But it wasn't. Every word of it was true. I packed my bags and walked out on him.

Marion Very sensible.

Laura Somehow he managed to find me. He had me taken to his house in Hampstead. It was like a prison. I was watched every minute of the day. I couldn't call anyone. I couldn't write. I was going out of my mind. At last I thought of a plan. I told him I thought I was pregnant. He was over the moon about it. Naturally I had to have the best, so he sent me to see a friend of his in Harley Street—under escort, of course. I managed to climb out of a window and gave them the slip.

Marion How very clever of you.

Laura I didn't know where to turn. That's when I thought of Dorothy Ledston. I managed to trace her through the agency she worked for and moved in with her until I got a chance to move out of London. When Andrew contacted her about looking after you, it was a golden opportunity. She agreed to let me take her place, loaned me her spare uniform and saw me on to the train. I can't tell you how nervous I was. If anyone had seen us together and recognized me, they'd have scarred her for life to find out where I'd gone. That's why I wore this wig. I promised I'd keep in touch with her through the agency—Christina Martins—but the day after, she failed to turn up for work. (*Quietly*) They found her the following week.

Marion Your gangster husband's work, I suppose?

Laura I don't know. I really don't know. But it wouldn't surprise me.

Marion And Andrew Thorne?

Laura (*forcing a smile*) My cousin. He promised to help me get out of the country. To America . . . Australia . . . somewhere Dave wouldn't be able to reach me. He was going to join me later. After you . . . (*She breaks off as she realizes*)

Marion After I'd conveniently died and left him all my money. Yes?

Laura (*faintly*) Excuse me. I'm not feeling well.

Marion No. I can see.

Laura (*shakily*) Would you mind if I sat down?

Marion Please do. (*She moves up to let Laura sit beside her*) Here. (*She hands her the untouched glass of brandy Katherine left*) Perhaps a sip of this will make a difference.

Laura Thank you. (*She sips the brandy gratefully*)

Marion (*after a moment*) You were saying?

Laura (*pulling herself together*) You can imagine how I felt when I heard the news. I was convinced she'd been killed because of me. And when Katherine found those cigarettes in the summer-house, I thought they'd managed to trace me. Unfortunately Christina rang while Katherine was still in the room. She'd been keeping me informed on what was happening up there. I couldn't think what to say, so I told that stupid lie about it being Mrs Meacham. (*She sips more brandy*)

Marion (*sighing*) Yes, that was unfortunate, wasn't it? It only increased her suspicions of you. I suppose that's the real reason you killed Michael, isn't it? To give her something else to worry about.

Laura (*desperately*) I didn't kill Michael. I didn't kill anyone.

Marion Then how did he get hold of the headscarf?

Laura (*heavily*) He did come here that night. Just as I was about to leave. He saw me without my wig and panicked when I snapped at him. I followed him out to the road, but he'd vanished. I was so furious I flung it away and drove off to meet Andrew. I never saw Michael again. I swear it. I was on edge all through dinner. That's why I crashed the car. Andrew will tell you. (*She retches violently*)

Marion (*thoughtfully*) So what you're saying is that Michael must have picked up the headscarf after you'd driven off?

Laura (*clutching her stomach in pain*) Yes. I suppose so. I don't know. (*She retches again*)

Marion (*rising unsteadily*) And your arrangement with Raymond?

Laura (*weakly*) Arrangement?

Marion To murder me.

Laura (*rallying*) There was no arrangement. He thought I was a murderess, too. He thought he could blackmail me into killing you in return for keeping quiet about my being here. I pretended to go along with him, and the minute he'd gone, I called Andrew. We met in Hanbury yesterday afternoon and told the whole story to the police. They'll be arriving here at any moment to fix up a recording device. That's why we wanted you out of the way. To save you from being upset.

Marion (*nodding*) A fascinating story. (*She smiles*) Unfortunately, I don't believe a word of it.

Laura It's the truth.

Marion I'm afraid I can't agree, Mrs Sanderson. The truth is on that cassette tape that Katherine is delivering to my solicitor tomorrow morning . . . together with my amended will. Andrew Thorne won't see a penny of my money. I've made quite sure of that. Now if you'll excuse me, I'll go to my room. I've no wish to die in the same place as you.

Laura Die? (*She stares at Marion without comprehension*)

Marion There were quite a number of crushed pills in the milk. The empty bottles will be found on my bedside table.

Laura (*attempting to rise*) You mean . . . you've poisoned me?

Marion I've poisoned us both, my dear. I couldn't permit you to live after what you've done, and I couldn't live with myself knowing what I'd done. Not even for a few more days. We've put a lot in common, haven't we? We've both killed twice.

Laura (*weakly*) No. No. (*She collapses back on the settee*)

Marion It'll be swifter for you, dear. Your body isn't used to the drug. But I won't be far behind. (*She moves to the door* R) Goodbye, Mrs Sanderson.

Laura (*very faintly*) No. No. No. (*Her voice tails away into silence and she sinks into sleep*)

Marion pauses, turns, looks back at Laura for a moment then frowns. She picks up the telephone and dials 999

Marion (*with an effort*) Hello? Hanbury police station? . . . This is Miss Bishop of Moor View. I understand you're supposed to be sending someone out here this evening to—— . . . Yes. Yes, of course. Thank you. . . . Yes. I see. They've already left. With me in a few minutes. . . . (*She sways slightly*) No, no. I'm not worried. I'm sure they will. I have every confidence in the British police. Thank you. (*She replaces the receiver slowly and looks at Laura's motionless figure in disbelief. Softly*) The truth. You were telling the truth.

The sound of a car is heard, off. It stops, doors slam

A few moments later, Andrew enters followed by Katherine

Andrew Sorry I've been such a time, but we've had some marvellous news.

Katherine (*eagerly*) They've found the man who killed Michael. He was one of the people at Gail Crosby's party. He'd had too much to drink and shouldn't have been driving anyway. He's admitted everything.

Marion stands as though turned to stone

Andrew Where's Laura? (*He sees her*) Just look at that. (*He grins*) Come on, sleepy-head. (*He crosses to her and shakes her*) They'll be arriving any time now. Laura? (*Frowning*) Laura? (*Suddenly anxious he examines her*) Laura? (*Quickly he checks her heartbeat and pulse*) Laura. (*He looks round in bewilderment*) She's *dead*. (*To Marion*) What happened to her? What happened? (*He rises*)

Katherine stares at the body wide-eyed. Marion looks at Andrew and begins to sob and shake soundlessly as——

—the CURTAIN *falls*

FURNITURE AND PROPERTY LIST

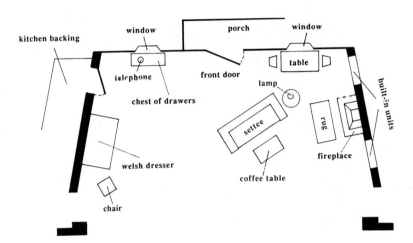

ACT I

SCENE 1

On stage: Drop-leaf table. *On it:* bowl of roses
2 chairs
Chest of drawers. *On it:* telephone, pen, address book, telephone directory
Welsh dresser. *On it:* silver tray with decanter and glasses
Dining-chair
2 built-in units. *On them:* television set, books, long-playing records, record-player
Fireplace. *On it:* small *objects d'art*
Rug
On walls: 2 paintings of the moor, framed pictures
Settee
Coffee table
Small table. *On it:* lamp, book
In porch: small table, coat-stand, Wellington boots, umbrella stand containing umbrella, trowel, plant pots, apple box

Off stage: Box of groceries **(Doris)**
White apron **(Katherine)**
Tray with 2 cups, saucers and biscuits **(Katherine)**
Doctor's case. *In it:* tourniquet **(Andrew)**
Blood 500 **(Michael)**
Towel **(Katherine)**
Shirt **(Katherine)**
Stick **(Marion)**

Personal: **Katherine:** wrist-watch (worn throughout)
Andrew: wrist-watch (worn throughout)
Raymond: wrist-watch (worn throughout), handkerchief in pocket
Marion: wrist-watch (worn throughout)

SCENE 2

Strike: Groceries' box
Tea-tray

Set: 2 cups and saucers
2 raincoats (on porch coat-stand)

Off stage: 2 suitcases **(Andrew)**
Tea-tray **(Katherine)**
Towel **(Andrew)**

Personal: **Laura:** wig (worn throughout)

SCENE 3

Strike: Tea-tray
Towel
Laura's coat

Set: Portable radio

Off stage: Tea-tray **(Marion)**
Scissors, bunch of flowers **(Laura)**
2 gift-wrapped packets. *In one:* packet of shortbread biscuits
Tea-tray **(Laura)**
Plate of biscuits **(Laura)**
Headscarf **(Laura)**
Doctor's case **(Andrew)**
Packet of cigarettes **(Katherine)**

ACT II

SCENE 1

Strike: Tea-trays

Set: Notebook and pencil

Off stage: 2 small bottles of tablets **(Laura)**
Glass of water **(Laura)**
Headscarf **(Laura)**
Cup and empty plate **(Stage Management)**

Personal: **Laura:** handbag. *In it:* small mirror

SCENE 2

Strike: Plate and cup

Set: Cassette-recorder

Off stage: Basket of apples **(Laura)**
Box of groceries **(Doris)**

Personal: **Raymond:** snapshots in pocket

SCENE 3

Strike: Cassette-recorder

Off stage: Manila package **(Laura)**
Tea-tray **(Laura)**

Personal: **Katherine:** headscarf and kitchen knife in pocket

LIGHTING PLOT

Practical fittings required: table lamp, pendant light

Interior. A living-room. The same scene throughout

ACT I, Scene 1

To open: Bright interior lighting, hot sunny exterior lighting

| Cue 1 | **Raymond** exits and we see him pass the window L
Black-out | (Page 12) |

ACT I, Scene 2

To open: Gloomy exterior lighting, table lamp on, fireglow from fireplace

| Cue 2 | Crash of thunder
Black-out | (Page 20) |

ACT I, Scene 3

To open: Bright interior lighting, hot sunny exterior lighting

| Cue 3 | **Katherine** slowly looks at door R
Black-out | (Page 30) |

ACT II, Scene 1

To open: Evening exterior effect, pendant light on

| Cue 4 | **Katherine** takes a book and begins to read
Slowly fade to Black-out; after a few moments return to original setting | (Page 39) |
| Cue 5 | **Laura** stands looking at **Doris** and **Katherine**
Black-out | (Page 40) |

ACT II, Scene 2

To open: Bright interior lighting, hot sunny exterior lighting

| Cue 6 | **Laura:** "He wants us to murder his aunt."
Black out | (Page 51) |

ACT II, Scene 3

To open: Evening exterior effect, pendant light on and fire glow from fireplace

No cues

EFFECTS PLOT

ACT I

Cue 18	**Laura:** "He's just arriving."	(Page 27)
	Sound of car approaching, it stops and door slams	
Cue 19	**Katherine** stands looking thoughtful	(Page 30)
	Telephone	

ACT II

Cue 20	To open SCENE 1	(Page 31)
	Music from radio	
Cue 21	**Katherine** picks up radio and exits	(Page 34)
	Slowly fade music	
Cue 22	**Laura** exits, closing the door behind her	(Page 35)
	Car door slams, then sound of car starting up and moving away	
Cue 23	A car door slams and car moves away	(Page 35)
	Telephone	
Cue 24	**Katherine:** "I'll explain everything to her."	(Page 38)
	Telephone	
Cue 25	**Katherine** is asleep on the settee	(Page 39)
	Sound of car approaching, it stops and door slams	
Cue 26	**Katherine:** "Oh, there was one thing, though——"	(Page 39)
	Sound of car approaching, it stops and door slams	
Cue 27	**Andrew** opens the front door	(Page 45)
	Sound of car approaching, it stops and door slams	
Cue 28	**Andrew** exits	(Page 45)
	After a pause, a car door slams and there is the sound of a car starting up and moving away	
Cue 29	**Laura** moves to the table and stands	(Page 47)
	A car door slams and the car moves away	
Cue 30	**Marion:** "Goodbye, dear."	(Page 57)
	After a moment, a car door slams and the car moves away	
Cue 31	**Marion:** "You were telling the truth."	(Page 62)
	Sound of car approaching, it stops, doors slam	

MADE AND PRINTED IN GREAT BRITAIN BY
LATIMER TREND & COMPANY LTD PLYMOUTH

MADE IN ENGLAND